BUY YOUR OWN BUSINESS WITH OTHER PEOPLE'S MONEY

Buy Your Own Business With Other People's Money

ROBERT A. COOKE

WILEY

John Wiley & Sons, Inc.

Published by John Wiley & Sons, Inc., Hoboken, New Jersey.
Published simultaneously in Canada.

For general information on our other products and services please contact our Customer Care Department
within the United States at (800) 762-2974, outside the United States at (317) 572-3993 or
fax (317) 572-4002.

Wiley also publishes its books in a variety of electronic formats. Some content that appears in print
may not be available in electronic books. For more information about Wiley products, visit our web site
at www.Wiley.com.

Library of Congress Cataloging-in-Publication Data:
Cooke, Robert A., 1931-
    Buy your own business with other people's money / Robert A. Cooke.
       p.   cm.
    Includes index.
    ISBN 978-0-471-69498-4 (pbk. : alk. paper)
    1. Business enterprises—Purchasing.   I. Title.
HD1393.25.C66 2005
658.1'62—dc22
                                            2004062618

10 9 8 7 6 5 4 3 2 1

CONTENTS

CONTENTS

Contents

CONTENTS

Contents

Be Your Own Boss— It's Not Just a Dream

You've listened to the pundits and you've read the books. They tell you that the road to being in business for yourself is long, hard, and requires vast quantities of cash to tide you over the start-up period or to buy an existing business. Some of that is true, some is myth, and it's often difficult to tell which is which. That's what this book is about—to help you sort through the chatter and determine how much cash you might need and where you can find people who will invest their money—not yours—in your business.

Most would-be entrepreneurs dream about, and the pundits talk about, starting a business from scratch. Why? On the surface, it appears that starting a business takes far less money than one would have to fork over to buy an existing business. That's the conclusion that would be reached by most people who read the business opportunities section of the classi-fied ads in the newspaper. But if a budding entrepreneur can leap over that problem about the initial cash, buying an existing business often makes far more sense. For instance, the present or some previous owner has gone through the turmoil of learning lessons from the trials and tribulations peculiar to a start-up. That means that advertising is well targeted to prospective customers, loyal customers have been developed, employees have been trained, and operating and accounting systems are in place. The buyer of the business saves all that development work. Of course, this assumes that the business is profitable. If you are looking for a business that is in chaos and distress and verging on bankruptcy, the seller of the business can hardly demand much if any up-front cash from a buyer.

That's why I wrote this book—to help people with a lot of ambition and energy, some experience and knowledge, and very little cash, to avoid the hassles of starting a business and, in a way, to enjoy the fruits of someone else's labor. (But the business will still demand much of your own.)

Where do people get the impression that buying a going business is an opportunity available to only the cash rich? It's from those heads in the newspaper. Think for a minute about your situation if you were selling a business. Wouldn't you put an ad in the paper that asks for a bunch of money right up front? Would you really expect to find a buyer who can write you a check for many thousands of dollars? That probably would not happen, so after a few weeks you lowered your expectations and listened to prospects who wanted to buy your business on the installment plan. As time dragged on, you might become so desperate that you would listen to proposals from not only those with no money, but also those who have substantial debt. In other words, you may have reached a stage where any possibility of eventually receiving substantial payments for your business is better than just shutting the door.

That's when you, as a buyer, can make your move to buying a business with little or no cash down.

Of course, there are many other sources of other people's money, such as lenders and investors, and there are still other sources that are well hidden until you look deeply within the business. This book should help you find those sources.

CHAPTER 1

The Good and the Bad of Owning Your Own Business

For most people, finding the money with which to buy a business is really Step Two. Step One is making some fundamental decisions about type of business, location, market, future demand for the product or service, and whether entering the world of an entrepreneur is right for you. Therefore, we start with a few thoughts to help you think through some important factors in buying a business. (If you have already made a decision on a specific business—for instance, you are going to buy Aunt Isabel's insurance agency or Uncle Harry's hardware store—you could skip directly to Chapter 2.)

Own your own business—it's a great American dream. If you look at the ads in various business magazines for franchises, you'll get the impression that being an entrepreneur is a sure way to riches beyond anything possible in your present job. If you take out the word "sure" and insert the word "possible" or "probable," you have what is generally a true statement.

Here are some considerations to think about in deciding whether your enterprise will be almost a sure thing or just a possibility.

The Fictions and the Facts about Owning a Business

There are advantages to owning a business, but in our thinking we often blow them up to be out of proportion to the disadvantages. These exaggerations often contain much that isn't true. That's why I use the term "fiction." They can be classified as follows:

- *No boss:* It would be wonderful to go to work knowing that it is you who gives the orders. No longer do you take orders.
- *Short hours:* There will be no one to look at the time clock if you arrive a few minutes late in the morning or leave early in the afternoon. In fact, you can take the whole day off and have to answer to no one.
- *Large income:* Now you can actually live in the manner to which you would like to become accustomed. A large home, the expensive automobiles, the yacht, and world travel are within your reach.
- *Prestige:* Being a business owner moves you into the upper reaches of society in your city or town.

And this can all be yours, if only you have the money with which to buy a business.

Fiction Number One: No Boss

In your present job, you may be annoyed by your supervisor if she micromanages your activities and questions nearly all your decisions. That is, she makes your working life intolerable. It is true that owning your business will relieve you of this sort of pressure, but you will now have a different form of boss: Your customers may make demands on you that are almost as insufferable as the dictator who formerly ran your life. And you'll have other bosses:

- Your local tax collector will collect various fees, such as business licenses.

- With few exceptions, your state tax collector will impose a series of bookkeeping procedures on you so that you can collect the sales tax from your customers.

- Various government entities will demand reports from you and inspect your facilities for compliance with health and safety rules, compliance with rules about compensation of employees (as regulations about overtime pay), and so on.

- Last, but not least, is the Internal Revenue Service (IRS). When you do make all that money, the IRS will have its hand out for a significant portion of it, and you will pay it to them, because that is less onerous than what happens if you don't. Also, the IRS will impose bookkeeping and recordkeeping requirements, for sending the taxes you and your employees owe, on time, to the IRS and probably to state tax authorities as well.

Fiction Number Two: Short Work Hours

It is true that some entrepreneurs manage to organize their businesses so that they run themselves, or at least they are run by dependable employees, making it unnecessary for the business owner to be on the premises except to review reports of operations or take care of an emergency. However, most entrepreneurs have these challenges:

- An employee does not show up for work, and there's no source for a substitute except the owner of the business. Most small entrepreneurs say they do everyone else's job, including cleaning the restrooms.

- Some jobs in a business's industry require in-depth knowledge and skills that make employees who can perform those jobs extremely expensive. When a business cannot afford to hire such employees, the owner must perform these tasks. This is particularly true of professional organizations, in which certain tasks must be performed, or at least reviewed, by licensed professionals.

- An entrepreneur has to spend considerable time in developing new business, such as calling on prospective clients and customers, buying advertising, schmoozing at Chamber of Commerce functions, or various other business-building activities.

Fiction Number Three: You Will Have Lots of Money

This is probably the biggest and meanest fiction of all. Yes, as your business grows, you'll see more cash come in the door (or electronically), but you will also see most of that cash go out the door for inventory, payroll, and other expenses. You get to keep just a small fraction of that cash flow, and as a business grows, you get to keep even less (or none) because of added payroll, the need for more space, and so on.

Suppose you open a booth at the local flea market or on eBay, from which you sell goose yokes. Sales average about 10 goose yokes per day, at a retail price of $10 each. In order to not lose sales because you are out of stock, you try to maintain an inventory of 15 goose yokes. The Goose Yoke Manufacturing Company is a short drive away, so you can purchase the yokes at wholesale daily (including weekends), but the manufacturing company's terms are cash at time of pickup. So, to have at least 15 goose yokes on hand every morning, you have to invest cash in your business with which to purchase your original inventory of 15 yokes at a wholesale price of $6 each, for a total investment of $90.

Then, next week, your sales increase to 20 yokes per day, which means the profit on your sales has increased by $40 (10 times the $4 profit on each yoke). But you can't take that $40 home, because now you need an inventory of 30 yokes, and at $6 each for the 15-yoke increase, you now have to spend $90 to increase your inventory. Not only do you not get to take the $40 home, you have to invest another $50 in order to buy the additional inventory you need.

This money that's invested in inventory is part of what's called *working capital*. The correct calculation of just how much working capital you'll need is critical when you look for money with which to buy a business, especially if that business will need a substantial increase in sales.

Fiction Number Four: You Will Enjoy the Prestige of Owning a Local Business

If prestige is important to you, you may find that it is one of the benefits of being a local entrepreneur. However, it won't happen right away. Initially, you'll be observed by those who already "have it made." They'll look at you as an unproven entrepreneur and, therefore, an unqualified competitor. But when you are financially successful and have the time and money to support civic and charitable causes, you can earn some prestige.

Do the Advantages of Entrepreneurship Outweigh the Disadvantages?

Basically, this is a decision that only you can make. If you are very unhappy in your present job because of an overbearing supervisor, or if your employer is too strict in the rules and regulations department, changing to another employer may answer your need. If that is not the case, use a time-tested method of dividing a letter-sized piece of paper vertically in half and listing the advantages of owning your own business in one column and the disadvantages in the other. That is your task. Neither I nor anyone else can do that for you, because only you know the details of what are important and unimportant to you.

Decide on the Type of Business That Is Best for You

Is your burning desire to be in business for yourself so strong that you will consider almost any legitimate business, or do you aspire to only one or two types of businesses? For instance, if your avocation is art (and you are a pretty good artist), your only desire may be to own and run an art gallery. If you are a computer geek, your only goal may be to operate a computer repair and maintenance business. In both cases, a different type of business holds little or no interest for you. On the other hand, you may be so fed up with corporate bureaucracy that you would move to any type of entrepreneurship as a means of escape from the corporate environment. (That's not to say you should not form your own corporation, but controlling a corporation and working for one are two different matters.) But these comments oversimplify the goal-setting process in seeking to become an entrepreneur, so let us examine some details of this decision process.

Determine Your Preference or Need as to Geographic Area

Do you like warmth and water sports, or do you prefer the snow and slopes—or do you enjoy both? Your preference can determine locality, but bear in mind you may not have much time to enjoy the climate during your initial involvement in your business. Some entrepreneurs avoid that dilemma by becoming involved in a seasonal business in which they put in the proverbial 18 hours per day, 7 days per week, for several months and then travel to alternate living in their preferred climate for the rest of year.

Medical problems (yours or those of a member of your family) may determine location or limit the choices of location. For instance, you may have allergies that you would like to escape, and only a warm, dry climate, as in Arizona, will help you.

Do not forget that moving to another city can be expensive. You need to consider not only the dollar cost of moving, but the cost of your time, the physical exertion of moving, making new contacts in your new area, and the emotional effect on other family members.

Consider the Hours of Operation

Another consideration is your biological clock. If you are a morning person and generally collapse into bed at 9:00 or 10:00 P.M., you should probably not consider owning and managing a nightclub that opens at about your bedtime and ceases its noise and confusion at 3:00 A.M. Similarly, if you're a night person and you plan on operating a breakfast and lunch restaurant that opens at 6:00 A.M. and closes at 3:00 P.M., you may find that resetting your biological clock will be a traumatic experience. This consideration becomes more important for an entrepreneur than it would for an employee because entrepreneurs tend to put in much longer hours (at least initially), so fitting those hours to your biological clock becomes more important.

Experience and Knowledge Are Important

You may be so upset with your current job in your current industry that you have decided you want a business far afield from your current experience. This could be a mistake. Your experience in your industry has value. This should be obvious, in that an employer in that industry will pay you substantially more than he would pay an entry-level person, simply because you have experience. For instance, if you have been working for a carpet-cleaning company, that experience would give you a head start in your run to success, but if you bought an auto-body repair shop, the carpet-cleaning experience could be of much less value.

That is not to say, however, that some experience does not translate into an advantage in operating almost any business. For instance, if you have been in a position in which you were responsible for hiring, firing, and training employees, you have experience that is transferable to almost any type of business.

Some businesses are inherently unsuitable for anyone who does not have the necessary experience. For instance, success in the computer maintenance and repair business demands that the owner have the knowledge and experience of a dedicated geek, preferably with some formal certification, such as Microsoft's A+ designation.

Pick a Business You Enjoy

Because you will be spending many hours at your business, it makes sense to do what you can to make at least some of those hours enjoyable. If your hobby is model railroads, owning a hobby store that specializes in these railroads may be your cup of tea. (However, be sure to locate in a populous area composed of people with above-average incomes!) Similarly, if you enjoy woodworking, look for a custom furniture shop with an established following.

There is a downside to this advice about seeking an enjoyable business. If a business is enjoyable, there will always be more competitors than there is market. The flip side is that if you buy a business that provides little enjoyment (such as a fat-rendering plant), you may find there is little competition in your area.

Also, be aware that some enjoyable hobbies may not lend themselves to enjoying the same hobby as a business. If your avocation is boating (sailing, fishing, cruising), owning a boatyard may look attractive, but the trials and tribulations of the business may keep you in the yard, not on the water.

Creating Your Experience

Once you have decided on a type of business (or businesses) that would meet your desires, you may be impatient to start looking for that ideal business and negotiating for its purchase. But are you sure about your decision? Try this. Go to work for someone in your desired type of business, even if it's for minimum wage. (If you're still employed, seek a part-time job in the industry, if that's appropriate.) For instance, if you're interested in the fast-food business, apply for the job of slicing French fries or waiting on customers at the front counter. Find out what that life is really like, and what sort of challenges are faced by the manager. You don't need to do this for long, for this is not the stage in which you devote a lot of time and money to investigating a type of business. That is covered later in this book.

CHAPTER 2

How Much to Pay (Borrow) to Buy a Business

Do not get your business so far in debt that you will never get out. Avoid surprises that can ruin your dream.

There are various tools that you can use to determine how much a going business is worth. Unfortunately, each tool will probably arrive at a different number, and the differences between the results will be significant. Here are the more common techniques.

How Much Is the Seller Asking?

Strictly speaking, this is not a valuation method, but rather the starting point for negotiation. As you talk to business sellers, remember that they probably have put in years of toil to build a business. Since they may have had a low income at the beginning, they feel that when they sell the business they should be compensated for those low-earning years. That's an understandable attitude, but it is not your job to compensate them for their sacrifices. It is your job to determine what the business is worth as it stands today. You should pay no more than that.

What Do Similar Businesses Sell For?

The answer to this question, in dollar terms, can provide a valuation figure. However, there are some drawbacks, or at least pitfalls, of which you should be aware.

- It is unusual to find two or more businesses that are practically identical in all respects, such as facilities, location, customer loyalty, employee stability, management acumen, and so on. (Franchised businesses, such as Jiffy Lube or Wendy's, are more likely to lend themselves to comparison, since the franchisor generally imposes operational rules that create look-alike, cookie-cutter businesses.)
- There may be clauses in the sales agreement of a similar business of which you are not aware. For instance, a similar business may have been sold for a lower price because the agreement also provided for additional payments to the seller if the business prospers under the new owner.
- If real estate is included in the sale of a similar business, the issue is how much of the price was for the real estate and how much for the business.
- A business that is located at an intersection that is a prime site for a shopping mall would sell for more than a similar business in a location with no such prospects, assuming both businesses included the underlying real estate.

What Is the Value of the Business's Assets?

You can value a business simply by determining the fair market value of the assets that are owned by the business. If you are buying a machine shop, you can take the position that the business is worth the value of the lathes, drill presses, and mailing machines, plus the office equipment, such as desks, chairs, and computers. If the business is not prospering, this may be a realistic value, since there may be no *going concern value*. Even at that, you're left with determining the fair market value of the equipment.

When we talk about the value of equipment, we have to clarify what we mean by "value."

Fair market value is the value of the equipment to someone who is going to use it in business. In other words, it's the price at which a buyer and seller, neither of whom are under pressure to complete the deal immediately, would agree to transfer the equipment from the seller to the buyer.

Distressed value or *liquidation value* is usually the price that can be obtained in a very quick sale, such as at a public auction. It is also the price at which a professional liquidation company would buy all of the equipment in one lot. If a business is closed or inoperative, and the owner is near bankruptcy, you may be able to acquire the business for liquidation value. (Find out why the present owner had to close the business—you may not want it at any price!)

Going concern value is generally the highest value, for it is the value of the equipment in an operating, profitable business. For instance, a used deep fryer by itself is worth only so much. But if it is part of a thriving business and operating satisfactorily, then it is worth more in its place, where it is happily cooking French fries for customers.

If you not only buy the assets of a business but also assume the liabilities, then you need to subtract the sum of those liabilities from the value of the assets. There is more on assuming liabilities of the seller in Chapter 3.

Value the Assets at Their Book Value

The word "book" in *book value* refers to the accounting records of the business. The term is a holdover from the days when all accounting records were maintained with pen and ink in large books containing ledger paper, with its columns and lines. In other words, whether the business maintains its records on the backs of old envelopes or with a computer makes no difference in computing the book value of an asset, and that value is usually the amount that the business paid for that asset, with some modifications. As we shall see, the book value of a business seldom reflects its true worth for various reasons.

The Book Value of Equipment

The book value of power saws, milkshake machines, automobiles, bulldozers, computers, and all other equipment is composed of two elements. The first is the amount that the business paid for the piece of equipment, and the second is the depreciation that has been recorded in the accounting records.

> For example, John is the owner of John's Machine Shop. When he started the business three years ago, he purchased all new equipment, which cost him $500,000. That cost is the number that goes on the books when the equipment is delivered. Then, John's accountant,

Notice the difference in meaning between the accountant's use of the term "depreciation" and the automobile salesman's use of the same term. To the accountant, the process of depreciation is simply spreading the original cost of the piece of equipment (as an automobile) over the expected life of the equipment. To the automobile salesman, it means the loss in value of your vehicle the moment you drive it out of the dealer's lot and the continuing loss in value as you drive the automobile for several years. It is the accountant's concept we use in computing book value.

Sarah Bell, depreciated that equipment over a five-year schedule, which means that in each of the five years she deducted $100,000 as depreciation expense and reduced the book value of the equipment by $100,000. Therefore, at the end of three years, the book value of the equipment is ($500,000 − $300,000) or $200,000.

The Book Value of Accounts Receivable

Accounts receivable generally refers to the money owed to the business for sales already made. Again, there is a concept of book value in valuing accounts receivable. For most small businesses, accounts receivable is simply the total of all the money that is owed to a business by its customers. However, as we are all aware, the world is full of people who have come upon misfortune (and some are outright deadbeats) who will never pay what is owed. Therefore, accounts receivable should be valued at something less than the book value. How much less depends on examining the list of receivables for old customers who have a payment history and will probably pay the amount owed. How new customers are valued will depend on the credit-granting policy of the business. If credit is extended to almost anyone, accounts receivable from those people should be reduced considerably. If credit reports are ordered on all new customers, a buyer can examine the credit reports and determine the probability that the business will be paid for the accounts receivable. At any rate, the book value of accounts receivable is a number that is different from market value.

Inventory

This is the hardest item to value in the purchase of assets, because inventory fluctuates daily for any company that is in business. If you are fortunate enough to be buying a business that already has the scanning and other equipment that is necessary for keeping perpetual inventory, you may find that pricing as of the day of the transfer of ownership is relatively simple. However, many small businesses value inventory by simply counting what's on hand and looking back through supplier invoices to determine how much each item cost. Obviously, this is a time-consuming process, and to be accurate it requires closing doors for one or two days, which is not a procedure that will endear you to customers.

You can set up a procedure for staying open during inventory if you note on a copy of each sales invoice whether the merchandise came out of stock before or after inventory of that item. Then adjust the inventory to deduct items sold after the inventory was taken of that item. The resulting figure should be the value of the inventory at the end of the day. This is a workable system if you're selling big-ticket items, such as furniture, but in a small-item business such as a sundry store, or a plumbing supply or hardware store, it's virtually impossible to take inventory without closing.

Also, check the inventory carefully as to both condition and obsolescence. Some small-business people refuse to sell anything for less than it originally cost the business, with the result that they may still have unused slide rules or typewriter ribbons on the office supply shelves.

Patents and Copyrights

If an invention or work of art has been developed internally in the business, then the book value may consist of just filing fees and the payments that were made to a patent or intellectual property attorney. In some businesses, the patent may be on a machine or process that is the mainstay of the business; therefore, the real value of the patent is many times the book value.

The Book Value of Other Assets

The other major asset is cash, and in this instance the book value is equal to the market value. (Realistically, a business that is something other than a corporation will be sold without any cash, since the owner may withdraw cash without tax consequences.)

If there are other assets listed in the balance sheet, such as prepaid expenses, intangible assets and other esoteric matters, you are well advised to engage a certified public accountant for the purpose of helping you decipher those terms and determine what the real value of those assets is.

The Asset Called *Goodwill*

If you're thinking of buying John's Machine Shop, you could look at the books and see that the only significant asset has a book value of $200,000. Therefore, you offer John $200,000 for his business. John would probably laugh, for at least two reasons. First, as we discussed, it would cost $700,000 to replace this equipment, and John's three-year-old equipment, we'll assume, would have a realistic market value of $350,000.

Secondly, John has built up a steady trade with equipment repair places, contractors, and other customers, as well as securing a government contract for machine shop services to a local Army base. So John would value his business as follows:

Equipment	$ 350,000
Customers' contracts and goodwill	650,000
Total price of business	$1,000,000

At this point then, we can define goodwill as the difference found by deducting the book value of the assets you are buying from the market value of those assets. (If you are not only buying the assets of the business but are also agreeing to pay off the liabilities of the business, the computation becomes a little more complex, as we will discuss later.)

Obviously, you cannot buy the business for the bargain price of $200,000. Although you and John both agree on the $350,000 as the value of the equipment, there's no reason you should accept John's estimate of the *goodwill* value of the existing customers.

How do you determine the value of the goodwill in a business? The usual procedure is called the *capitalization of earnings*.

The Capitalization of Earnings

Think about what you are really buying when you buy a business. Yes, you are buying equipment, fixtures, inventory, and perhaps the building to house all that stuff. But are you buying this to have it around, just as you might buy a Picasso to hang over your fireplace? Probably not, unless you're independently wealthy and buy a small business so you can claim to be self-employed and complain about work along with the rest of us. Most of us buy a business because it's a means of generating at least an above-average income, so the value of the business is based on how much income it generates.

Important: Please note that the starting point of this valuation method is to determine how much income the business currently generates. This is not an assumed figure of how much the business might generate under your capable management. In other words, the seller should not have any claim on future earnings of the business once ownership has transferred.

How to Determine the Real Net Income of a Business

Computing the earnings of a business is not a matter of simply looking at the income statement or the tax return of the business as prepared by, or for, the current owner. The earnings of the owner cloud this issue, and the precise sort of cloudiness depends on the legal form of the business. If you are not an accountant or a financial analyst, I suggest you review the information you receive from the present owner with a financial professional. (Do not ask for advice and suggestions from the same financial professional who provides services to the seller of the business, but you might contact that person to answer questions about how items on the financial statements were computed.) What follows is a list of the challenges that can arise in this area.

- The business is operated as a *sole proprietorship*. This is the form of doing business that happens by default when an individual starts providing services or sells merchandise to other individuals or companies. On a financial statement, you should find an item on the balance sheet, in the equity section, stating that *owners draw* was some dollar figure. The common error is to assume that this is the income that the business earned during the year, but such is not the case. For instance, if a business earned $200,000 during a year and the owner drew out only $80,000 for his or her personal use, there would be $120,000 of earnings left in the business. If in the following year (the year just before you are making an offer on the business), the business again earns $200,000 and the owner takes a draw of $250,000, the owner has taken a draw that is more than the business earned in this second year. So ignore this draw figure and look at the income (or profit and loss) statement on which you will find total sales, total costs, and total expenses. Don't worry about accountants differentiating between costs and expenses—they both reduce the sales figure to arrive at net income (earnings).

- The business is operated as a *partnership*. The computation of net income is computed just the same as for a sole proprietorship. That is, you should look at the income statement and not at the draws that may be withdrawn from the partnership in various amounts by the individual partners. Watch out for the following technicalities. Some payments to partners may be labeled "guaranteed payments" or "partner's salary" and deducted as an expense. Since these are actually payments to the owners of the business, they should be removed from the computation of total expenses and added to the bottom line that is the income shared by the partners. (This is the same concept that will be discussed later for corporations and salaries paid to stockholders.)

- The business is operated as a *limited liability company (LLC)*. The bookkeeping and tax return for an LLC are almost identical to those for a partnership. The confusing difference is that people who are partners in a partnership become members if the partnership changes to the LLC form.

- The business is operated as a *corporation*. There are more computations to make in this situation, since an owner of a corporation (a stockholder or shareholder), if he or she is active in the business, should be paid a salary by the corporation. That salary is an expense to the corporation, so its bottom-line income is less than it would be if the business operated as a sole proprietorship or partnership. To make the corporation comparable to these other forms of business, you have to remove the owners' (stockholders') salary from the expense category and add it onto the net income of the corporation. Then the figure for net income would better reflect the total earnings of the corporation. (See the sidebar on owners' salaries.)

Most small-business owners are not trained as accountants or bookkeepers, so the computation of net income may involve significant errors, and this makes it difficult to use current earnings as a basis of valuation.

There is an alternative way, which is preferred by many consultants, of computing the net income of a business. It consists of eliminating the salaries of the owner, partners, or corporate stockholders from the expense category and adding them to the bottom-line profit. Then, assume that you will hire a qualified manager to run the business for you. Deduct the manager's salary from the new profit figure to determine a net profit that the business would earn for you as an owner. Of course, since you will also serve as the paid manager, your total take-home pay will be composed of both the manager's salary and the profit. (Note that this is a way of envisioning the computation. Only if you have a corporation do you actually pay yourself a formal salary.)

For example, Danielle wanted to purchase Mickey's janitorial service. A summary of Mickey's corporation showed these figures:

Total sales		$1,000,000
Subtract expenses:		
Mickey's salary	$250,000	
Other expenses	725,000	
Total expenses		975,000
Net income		$ 25,000

At first glance, Danielle was not interested in a business that earned only $25,000. However, she made this calculation: to the $25,000 of profit she added Mickey's salary of $250,000 to arrive at a total of Mickey's take of $275,000. From a contact in the human resources discipline, she was able to determine that she could hire a manager for this business for $100,000 per year. Deducting that figure from the total of Mickey's take of $275,000 leaves a net profit of $175,000 for Danielle. That made the business considerably more attractive.

Nevertheless, this calculation should be part of your valuation computations unless you are sure that the financial statements or tax returns are pure fiction.

Would you believe it? Some small-business owners do cheat on their income tax computations by not reporting all of their sales or other revenue! Of course, that is illegal, and the penalties that the IRS may impose for this illegal procedure are substantial. (In some cases such tactics can lead to criminal prosecution and jail terms.) This tactic of cheating the government ends up actually cheating these business owners. If they have resorted to underreporting income from the business, the business will appear to be worth less. That can be an advantage to you as a buyer in negotiations. (If you have a relative or friend who works for the IRS, you might let that information slip early in the negotiations. If the seller has any common sense, that will prevent him from trying to justify a higher price by claiming that not all earnings were reported on the tax return and/or financial statements.)

You may find situations in which the reverse is true. That is, the business owner inflates his or her income figures to some fictitious amount. Yes, that means that the business pays some unnecessary income tax, but the owner hopes that the bookkeeping fiction will net many extra dollars when the business is sold.

If you are suspicious about the financial information the seller provides, you could engage an independent certified public accountant to audit the financial statements of the business. However, that's a lengthy, time-consuming process, for which the fees will run into thousands or tens of thousands of dollars, and these costs may not be reasonable in relation to the size of the business you are purchasing. Instead, ask your accountant to look through the bookkeeping records and advise of any material errors she spots, without rendering any opinion on the financial statements.

As a further procedure, look at the lifestyle of the business seller. Does it match the stated income? If the owner provides copies of tax returns that report $40,000 per year income but lives in a million-dollar home and drives an Aston Martin, ask for an explanation. If another seller lives in a small bungalow and drives a 10-year-old car, but reports an annual income from the business of $250,000, do some checking. In this instance, the latter seller may be investing much of this personal income. If his or her game is real estate, you can check that out at the courthouse or real estate tax collector's office. If she makes other investments, verifying the income is not so easy, but at least start by asking questions.

Determine the Price of a Business Based on Its Earnings (Income)

Although this book is about using other people's money to purchase a business, we discuss the source of the money after arriving at a valuation of the business. For that reason, and because it makes computation easier, we temporarily will assume you're using your own money to buy the business, even if your personal resources actually amount to $1.38.

Let us assume that you are looking at a business for which the owner is asking $1 million. The annual financial statements indicate the net income is $150,000 per year. Let's say you are currently employed in a management job with an annual salary of $90,000. So, you will earn $60,000 more than you are now making. Is that increase in income worth an investment of $1 million? Here is how to answer that question.

- From the annual owner's income from the business ($150,000), subtract the present salary of the buyer ($90,000); the difference ($60,000) is the increase in income the buyer would have if he or she bought the business.

- For that additional income, you, as the buyer, have to put up $1 million.

- Then, look at the alternatives available to you, the buyer. You could invest that $1 million in a conservative mutual fund composed of high-rated bonds and blue chip stocks. Over the years, such a fund should average earning at least 6 percent, or $60,000 on that $1 million investment. And all you had to do was keep your present job and write a check to the mutual fund, whereas managing a business can create a lot of hassles and certainly is not relatively risk-free.

Of course, if your present job is flipping burgers for $15,000 a year, this business would increase your income by $135,000. To someone in those circumstances, the business could be more attractive.

At this point, your comment is probably to point out that this book is supposed to show you how to buy the business using other people's money, and *that* is what this book should do. However, when you use other people's money, most such maneuvers entail the repayment to those other people sometime down the road (assuming the business is successful). So, the purchase price of the business will eventually come out of your pocket; even though the business may pay those other people, it will still leave less in the pot for you, as the owner, to take home.

When you talk to business brokers and financial people about valuing a business based on the earnings of the business, they will throw out two important terms: *capitalization of earnings* and *return on investment*.

Capitalization of Earnings and Return on Investment

Return on investment is the net income or profit that is earned by a business as a percentage of the owners' investment in the business. This is not unlike owning a share of stock or a certificate of deposit (CD). If you own a $1,000 CD that pays you $50 a year, your return on investment is 5 percent.

Capitalization of earnings is the reverse of the return on investment. If you want a return on your investment of 5 percent, how much do you need to invest to earn $50 per year? The answer is $1,000. (You multiply the required income by the rate of return you require.)

Obviously, since you could earn 5 percent in a risk-free investment, you should earn a much higher return on an investment in your own business, which does involve risk factors, some of which you can't control, such as weather, government meddling, general economic conditions, war, and so on. In my opinion, the purchase of any small business that returns anything less than 25 percent is foolhardy, unless there are other factors. (Do not forget to deduct a reasonable salary figure for yourself before computing the return on investment.)

What follows are step-by-step reviews of how to compute actual earnings and capitalization of those earnings. For those who like formulas, the steps are also expressed that way.

Method 1. This is like the previous example. The answer to the computation will vary depending on the current salary of the buyer in her present job:

Start with the current annual income of the business.

Add the seller's salary from the business, if that is deducted in computing profit.

Subtract the buyer's present salary.

Divide the resulting figure by the price of the business, to determine the return on investment in the business.

If you like formulas, the whole process can be expressed this way:

(Current income + seller's salary – buyer's present salary)
÷ price of business = return on investment in the business

Method 2. This is the more common method, since it does not depend on the buyer's present salary and therefore does not vary from buyer to buyer.

Start with the current annual income of the business.

Add the seller's salary from the business, if that is deducted in computing profit.

Subtract what it would cost to hire a manager.

Divide the resulting figure by the price of the business to determine the return on investment in the business.

Again, if you like formulas, the process can be expressed this way:

(Current income + seller's salary – what it would cost for a hired manager)
÷ price of business = return on investment in the business

If the business has borrowed money (as in financing new equipment) and includes the interest expense and expenses of the business, that generally should also be added to current income along with the owner's salary, unless you are assuming the liabilities when you buy the business.

When you have this return-on-investment figure for each business you are considering, it becomes relatively easy to compare their profitability relative to the investment required. You can now use various rules of thumb as to what return various businesses should generate. (The riskier the business, the higher the return should be.) Certainly, because of the risk involved in a small business, the return on investment should be at least 20 percent for any business and, preferably, much higher.

The Sales Multiplier

This is a shorthand method of valuing a business that is quick, but grossly inadequate. It states the value of the business as some number times its monthly sales. For instance, small restaurants may be valued at three or four months' sales; drugstores might sell for three months' sales; and some professional practices might be valued as high as one year of income. Obviously, just using sales as a basis on which to value of a business completely ignores the bottom-line profit. Some sales are profitable, and some are not, so it's obvious that the seller of a business could greatly increase the so-called value of his business by cutting his prices to the bone, heavily advertising that fact. That should increase sales by several times and thereby increase the rule-of-thumb value of his or her business. The moral is: Don't use these rules of thumb, but rely on the capitalization of earnings (if you have valid financial statements from the seller).

Third-Party Information

By now, it should be apparent that there is no easy way to value a small business, short of having a CPA audit the financial statements. Unless you are spending well into seven figures for a business, the cost of such an audit is prohibitive. However, information from people other than the seller can help you arrive at a fair market value of the business. (Some of these suggested procedures under this heading are procedures that the CPA would use in conducting an audit.)

Solicit Information from Employees of the Business

This action should be done first, since it is best performed before you make it known that you are interested in buying the business. This is relatively easy to do with a retail business, since you simply act as if you are a possible customer and engage the employees in informal conversation. Obviously, at this point it would be difficult to ask employees a laundry list of questions, but in casual conversation try for information such as:

- Is the business a good place to work? The answers to this question will obviously be biased, but can be of interest.

- Is there an adequate number of employees to provide expected service to customers?

- Are inventory levels adequate to meet customer demands? In other words, if the business is constantly out of stock, it probably has a cash-flow problem and marginal profitability.

- Do customers frequently leave without purchasing a product or service? This could indicate several problems, such as rude employees, inventory shortages, or prices unjustifiably higher than the existing competition. This could also indicate a competitive situation in the locality that might make the business unattractive.

- Is equipment in good working order? From the carpet cleaning business to the excavation contractor, failure to maintain and replace equipment as necessary may indicate a lack of profitability.

- Listen carefully to what employees say; there may be kernels of embedded information in their general conversation.

Note my references to cash-flow problems. While this can be an indication of lack of profitability of the business, that is not always the case. For instance, suppose that a business owner whose business is well capable of supplying him or her $100,000 a year wants to live like his neighbor who earns $200,000 a year. Before you sign on the line to buy any business, determine what income you must have to live adequately. If the business can provide that income, it may be a viable business, even if the present owner sucks too much money out of it. (Put off the Lamborghini, the yacht, and the airplane until later.)

Check the Bank Statements

Obtain copies of the bank statements for the last two or three years, and peruse the deposits made to the bank account for any abnormal variations. Also, add up the deposits for each year and compare that total to the total income on the income statement or a copy of the tax return provided by the seller. The seller should be able to explain, with documentation, any abnormal or significant differences between the totals from the bank statements and the figures on the income statement.

Can You Trust a Copy of the Business Tax Return?

It used to be that you had to trust whatever the seller provided in the way of a copy of income tax returns of the business. Now, however, the seller can request the IRS to send a "transcript" of his or her filed tax return to some party other than the taxpayer. Ask the seller to have such a transcript sent directly to you from the IRS, thereby assuring you of the veracity of the figures on it. (The request is made on a Form 4506. It is not necessary to use a tax professional to file this form, but using one may make sure the form is properly completed, which will expedite the process.)

If the business is a corporation, partnership, or LLC, the seller should not object to this request. However, if the business is organized as a sole proprietorship, the business return is an integral part of the whole individual tax return of the seller, so you may meet resistance to a request for a transcript of tax returns from a sole proprietor.

When Real Estate Is Part of the Business

When real estate that houses the business is sold along with the business itself, evaluation becomes somewhat more complex. Indeed, the price asked for a business may be unreasonable when computed by any of the methods we have discussed, except that the price includes valuable real estate. Perhaps the best example of this is the storage unit rental business, by which I mean those ubiquitous rows of shedlike buildings composed of individual storage units that anyone can rent and use as a place to keep extra stuff. As you may have noticed, these units are often located on busy thoroughfares where the land is more valuable than is needed for storage. What is happening is that the owner is holding the land as a speculative investment and, while waiting for the value to increase, operates a storage unit business on that land. The profits on the storage business help to defray the cost of holding that land, such as property taxes and the interest on the money invested in the land.

One way to determine the value of a business in this situation is to treat it as two separate businesses: the first is the operating business, and the second is the ownership of the real estate. Compute evaluation in this way:

- Obtain an appraisal of the real estate (land and buildings) by a qualified independent appraiser, and specify that the appraisal should include a fair rental value of the real estate.
- Deduct the appraised value of the real estate from the asking price of the business to determine the asking price of just the business alone.
- Using the capitalization of earnings method of valuation, determine if the business, without the real estate, will provide a reasonable rate of return to you.
- If this computation indicates you should buy the business with its real estate, be aware that you are also making a real estate investment, so part of your overall long-term income from the business will depend on how much the real estate appreciates over a period of years.

In Summary, the Eight Methods of Valuing a Business

1. The asking price (may be way overstated)
2. Comparison of the price for this business to prices for other similar businesses

3. Value of equipment included with business
4. The book value (may or may not reflect real value)
5. Capitalization of the profits of the business
6. Sales multiplier (generally not accurate)
7. Third-party information
8. Including the value for any real estate as part of the price

CHAPTER 3

Sources of Money for Your Business

There are many sources of cash for buying a business, some of which are obvious (your rich Aunt Sarah) or are the subject of circulating folklore (the Small Business Administration). We will discuss those, but first we will look at a prime source that is often overlooked—the seller of the business.

Borrow the Purchase Price from the Seller

Businesses are frequently sold for little or no cash down. Most sellers of a business eventually become aware of the real world, in which few people have the cash to purchase a business. That means that accepting future payment terms will make the sale of the business happen much sooner.

The "Business for Sale" Ads

"Business for sale with no money down." Did you ever see an ad with that heading? I never have, and I doubt that you have, unless it's some kind of scam. But many businesses are actually sold for little or no money up front.

Of course, everyone would like to sell products or services for cash. When an individual or a company receives cash in exchange for its product, the sale is complete, and the seller has immediate access to the cash. Who wouldn't want to try to get cash when they sell their business? In the real world, though, most buyers don't have cash. In the everyday flow of goods and services, people don't carry around much cash, often because they don't have any. For instance, Wal-Mart would love to sell on a cash-only basis, but how many sales would it lose? How many people would walk through Wal-Mart stores if they didn't accept payment by credit card? That means that the store does not receive the full price marked for the product, but some lesser amount. The difference, obviously, is the profit made by the credit card company.

This same situation applies to sellers of a small business. Of course, the seller would like to receive cash, and many sellers will stick to the "cash only" terms for a while. But then they'll find that buyers don't have cash, or at least they are unwilling to spend their own cash, so the sellers become more flexible. Then sellers have a choice: They can either sell their business for a cut-rate bargain price and receive mostly cash in exchange, or they can receive a reasonable price for the business by arranging extended payment terms for the buyer.

Archie negotiated a deal when he purchased a coffee and doughnut bar in the downtown financial district. The seller, Burt, advertised his business for sale for $100,000 with the notation that it must be "all cash." Archie's first offer to Burt was for $5,000 down with monthly payments of $3,000 until the balance of $95,000 was paid. Burt brushed off the offer as ludicrous and refused to negotiate anything other than a cash sale. Archie bided his time, frequently traveling by the coffee bar where he saw the aging Burt looking more and more weary as he actively managed the business. After three months of watching, Archie approached Burt with an offer of $10,000 up front. Again, Burt would not accept that, but he did indicate a willingness to be flexible on the all-cash demand to the extent that he might accept future payments if half of the $100,000 was paid in cash. To make a long story short, Archie and Burt continued to spar over the negotiation and one year later ended up with this deal: Archie would pay a down payment of $10,000 with payments in the original amount of $3,000 per month. However, the number of payments would be extended to cover interest at 10 percent, plus the total price that Archie would pay for the coffee bar was raised to $120,000. Also, Burt would be available as a consultant for a period of 12 months.

You no doubt have some questions about this deal. (You should have questions about any deal that is in its proposal stage.) Among them are these:

- Would it not have been less expensive for Archie to borrow the entire $100,000 from his local banker? In terms of the number of dollars involved, it probably would have been. However, Archie did not have strong enough credit that would have allowed him to borrow that amount of money without it being secured by some device, such as a second mortgage on his home or a lien on some other asset such as his yacht, airplane, or RV. (Actually, Archie does not have a yacht, airplane, or RV.) It would be foolish for Archie to tie up the equity in his home at this stage. He might need that source for additional financing if some tragedy, such as a hurricane, forced him to suspend business for a few weeks.

- Will it be impossible for Archie to "make it" if he overpays for the business by $20,000? That is a possibility, but Archie did his homework and has a solid basis for believing that the figure of $120,000 is still within his computations of a reasonable price.

The Seller's Motivation to Sell

If you know, or can find out, what motivates the seller, you will have an advantage in the negotiations for buying the business with little or no cash down. For this reason, it's a good idea to make an exploratory visit to the seller and the premises before constructing an offer to purchase. (If you can do this without revealing the fact that you may be interested in buying the business, so much the better.) The most common reasons for selling a business fall into these classifications:

- The owner wishes to retire. Depending on his or her age, the seller may or may not be strongly motivated. For instance, sellers in their early fifties have many years of healthy living ahead of them. While retirement is attractive, it is attractive only if they have adequate funds, and having those adequate funds may be very important in the sale of their business. In other words, they are not likely to be flexible on price, but they may be flexible on payment terms. Because the sellers are comparatively young, they are in a position to accept a payment schedule. That's because if the buyer defaults, the sellers can repossess the business and operate it until they find another buyer.

- The owner has found what she thinks is a better opportunity in the working world. This situation can mean that the seller, even if relatively young, is very anxious to sell. This anxiety may extend to accepting any reasonable payment plan.

- The owner is in ill health. This is obviously an unfortunate situation. You may feel averse to taking advantage of it, but consider this: If the business has been for sale for several weeks or months with no buyer in sight, the business may be sliding quickly downhill and soon will become worthless. Therefore, you are indeed doing the seller a favor by making any reasonable offer, including extended payment terms.

- The owner has died. This is the ultimate in unfortunate situations, but it does inevitably occur. If a family member or other heir is capable of operating the business, there may be little incentive to sell at anything less than a high price. If there is no one like this available to manage the business, the motivation to sell may be very strong. However, depending on whether or not the business owner planned ahead for his demise, the ability of the owner's estate to accept future payments may be nonexistent. At least, that's what the executor or administrator of the estate may say. Receiving cash for the business makes it easier to divide up the estate among the heirs and wind up the estate. Bear in mind, though, that the executor or administrator usually could settle the estate by accepting promissory notes in various denominations, which could be distributed among the heirs in the same manner as cash could be distributed. In other words, if you are rebuffed by the executor or administrator, wait a few weeks and submit another offer for payment terms. Of course, there's always a risk that during those few weeks someone else will show up who can pay the full cash price, but if you've been turned down initially, it will cost you very little in time and effort to resubmit your offer later.

■ The urge to sell is just a notion: Some business owners continuously keep their business discreetly listed at a very high price with business brokers. They are not willing to negotiate or accept future payments; they are just hoping to catch the not-too-astute buyer with more money than sense.

Enticing the Business Owner to Sell to *You*

Naturally, an astute seller will not sell to just anyone on a payment plan. Be aware of that fact in constructing an offer to a seller of a business. By that, I mean that the seller, if she accepts a promissory note from the buyer, wants to sell to someone who has a very high probability of being a success in the business and being able to make the note payments on time. To that end, your offer to purchase a business with little or no money down should include some background material on your management experience and previous successes. If you're short on management experience and a success history, make the offer anyway and try to include something positive that will impress the seller. This could be your situation if you're young and a recent graduate, but in that case you may have letters of recommendation from part-time/summer employment, internships, or work for charitable organizations. Of course, use your verbal skills to supplement your written materials. Remember that the worst nightmare of anyone selling a business is that the buyer will fail to make the payments and that ownership will revert to the seller. By that time, the business may have been run down, and the seller will have to work double time to restore profitability and make the business attractive to another buyer.

For more ideas on what to include in any no-money-down proposals to the seller of a business, see the following sections on proposals to com-

When I talk about a proposal or offer to purchase a business, the implication is that the proposal should be in written form. However, the negotiation certainly should start with an informal conversation, which sets some parameters as to price and other terms. Also, this preliminary conversation is your opportunity, as a cashless buyer, to impress the seller with your experience, education, and other qualifications that would assure that the business would prosper and be able to make any agreed-upon payments to the seller. Keep in mind that you are not only buying the business but selling yourself as a credible source of future payments. Reinforce your sales effort by including, in or with a written offer, a synopsis of your credentials.

As in any sales situation, try to find the business owner's hot button and talk about her interests (sports, music, entertainment, etc.).

mercial banks and venture capitalists. (When the seller finances the sale of the business as we're discussing, she assumes two roles: she is both the seller and the lender. Fortunately, as a lender, the seller is far more motivated to accept greater risks than is a commercial bank, venture capitalist, or other third party.)

Find Cash Inside the Business

You, as the buyer, may be able to find an immediate source of cash within the business. I suppose you might discover an old mattress in the basement of a store and find it full of cash the owner has forgotten about. That's not very likely. What is more likely are the following opportunities.

The Equipment Owned by the Business

The business may have equipment that has been fully paid for and is available as collateral for a bank loan.

> Paula was negotiating the purchase of a paving company that was owned by Shawn. All that stood in the way of the purchase was Paula's need for another $20,000 to swing the deal. In desperation, Paula reviewed all of the paperwork that had been generated by the negotiations and found a gem that had been overlooked. A road grader that the company owned had been paid off several months previously. Since this used piece of equipment had a fair market value of $40,000 and Paula had a reasonably good credit history, she was able to borrow that additional $20,000 from her local banker by using the grader as collateral.

The moral of this story is that when you consider buying a business, look carefully at the financial statements (particularly the balance sheet) as well as at the actual equipment the business owns. You may find something under the tarpaulin in the storage room that has value and can generate money from within the business.

There are other ways to use equipment as a source of funds to buy a business. If you know, or if you can meet, high-income individuals, approach them with the suggestion of a sale and leaseback.

> Donna was attempting to purchase a landscaping business, and that business owned a backhoe that would be worth $40,000 on the used equipment market. She convinced Dr. Chop to buy the backhoe from the business for $40,000 and lease it back to the business for $1,400 a month. Dr. Chop would not only receive the profit on the lease of

about $10,000 over three years, but he would have healthy depreciation deductions that would reduce his taxable income from his practice. The seller would receive a $40,000 down payment, and Donna would have bought the business. Of course, the sale and leaseback and closing on the business have to happen at the same time. (Let an accountant work out the actual depreciation figures.)

An alternative method of obtaining cash out of this piece of equipment—and this could work along with the sale and leaseback on the same equipment—is an equipment-sharing or time-share arrangement. While the landscape business uses a backhoe frequently, most of the time it sits idle by the office. Meanwhile, Ralph, who also owns a landscaping business, does not have a backhoe and frequently has to rent one. Donna could offer Ralph a time-share arrangement by which he would have the use of the backhoe 50 percent of the time for a monthly rental of $1,000. Then, to generate more immediate cash, she could offer Ralph a discount of 20 percent if he paid the first year's rental up front.

If none of those tactics work, Donna could always sell the backhoe and rely on renting one when she needed it. Admittedly, this is not the best alternative, but when you're buying a business with no money of your own, flexibility is the word.

A variation of the sale and leaseback can be used in purchasing any business with much expensive equipment. It works like this: The seller of the business keeps title to the equipment and leases it to you. Since you are not buying the equipment, the price of the business is lower, and your need for other sources of financing is less. The advantage to the seller is that he or she has a steady cash flow from the rentals of the equipment and still has title to the equipment, so he is well protected against the possibility of the buyer defaulting on the payments.

Intangible Assets

Generally, intangible assets are not a good source of financing. However, they can be used as described in the previous paragraph. That is, if a substantial portion of the price for the business is for patents and trademarks, negotiate for the seller to keep title to those items and license them to you for a monthly fee. The advantages and disadvantages are the same as for the situation in which the seller of the business maintains title to equipment (often called the *hard assets*).

Accounts Receivable

In many industries, accounts receivable can be *factored*. That is, a *factoring company* will buy the accounts receivable, advancing immediate cash to the business and then collect the cash from the customers who owe the business money as those receivables become due. Of course, the factoring company is not a nonprofit charity. It will pay the business something less than the face value of the receivables, and the difference between the two amounts is the profit for the factoring company. In some cases, the profit for the factoring company will seem unduly large, but if the arrangement swings the deal, it may be well worth it.

How do you find a factoring company? Typing the words "factoring" and "finance" into a search engine window should bring up several possibilities. I do not offer a specific recommendation for two reasons. First, I have not been involved with a company to use factoring for several years; and second, some factoring companies specialize in certain industries, so making a recommendation in a book that is not industry-specific is not possible. Another suggestion is that the trade association of the industry of the business you are buying may have some suggestions. It goes without saying that you should check out the reputation of the factoring company by asking for the names of current customers and following up on the references.

Historically, one of the downsides of factoring is that your customers have to remit payments directly to somebody other than you. Some factoring companies handle this more delicately than others, so be sure to check that out and read the factoring agreement that they ask you to sign. Also, be sure to determine whether the factoring company takes a risk of bad debts or if you have to make a refund to them for the debts of customers who do not pay.

Excess Inventory

Suppose you're looking at an upscale clothing store in an older neighborhood where the shopping district is filled with antique and art stores. While the store enjoys some loyal customers from the immediate neighborhood, most of the old customers have migrated to other neighborhoods and shop in the malls. The reduced volume of sales makes the store available, and you would like to buy it and move it into the mall along with its customers. In the meantime, the present owner has maintained a high inventory, which makes sense for the volume the store once did, but is far in excess of the needs for the current sales volume. In other words, the excess inventory could be an immediate source of cash.

To get at that cash, you could ask the seller to hold a sale at substantially reduced prices and sell off the excess inventory. If the inventory, at cost, was worth $150,000 and the sale sold off $50,000 of that inventory at cost, the seller would have the cash he or she wanted up front, the retail customers would get a whale of a deal, and now you could buy the business for $50,000 less. Offer to help the seller by waiting on customers during the sale. You may learn that there are reasons other than location for the diminishing sales, such as long delays in getting alterations completed or other unresponsive service. In that case, you may want to change plans. Instead of moving the store, you may want to open a mall location as a branch in the near future.

If the sale is not an option, call on other clothing stores who handle similar merchandise. Offer the excess inventory at 10 or 15 percent below current wholesale prices. Promise delivery of this merchandise (on C.O.D. terms) immediately upon becoming the new owner of your store. Admittedly, you won't generate as much cash this way, but if the arrangement enables you to purchase the business, it's probably well worth it.

Will you have to scrimp and live on beans and rice in order to build the inventory back up? Probably not, if you've included in your business plan the purchase of scanning equipment and software to maintain a lean inventory with automatic reorder points.

Actual Cash in the Business

It is unusual but not beyond reason to find significant cash in the business bank account. If the business is incorporated, the seller may be reluctant to take that cash out of the business, since it may generate a burdensome income tax bill. If that's the case, offer to buy all of the outstanding stock with the corporation's cash as part of the closing. This probably will still generate a tax bill for the seller, but it may be at long-term capital gain rates. (The proceeds to the seller would generally be long-term capital gain or dividends, which rates, at this writing, are both a maximum of only 15 percent. However, tax rules can and do change frequently, so an astute seller will seek advice from a qualified tax professional. However, if the seller of the business you want is amenable to structuring the sale as a means of withdrawing funds from the business, using the corporation's cash may appeal to him or her, and provide you with the funds you need to make the purchase.)

Personal Assets That Can Generate Cash

Personal assets can be used as collateral for borrowing funds. While it may seem that that is the same as using your own money, you are really using the bank's money. Because your business generates profits well beyond the salary rate of your present job, the business will pay back the bank and your home or other collateral will still be yours. Look at these areas for sources of cash:

- *Equity in your personal residence.* As you are no doubt aware, even though you have a first mortgage on your residence, if you have owned the property for several years and are in a good location, increasing real estate values plus the payments you have made have generated an equity in your residence. This is, of course, computed by deducting the principal balance of the mortgage from the market value of the property at the present time, and if you generally pay your bills on time, you should be able to borrow that equity amount (by signing a second mortgage note) at a reasonable rate from a mortgage company, a bank, a credit union, or some other financial institution. As an alternative, you could refinance the first mortgage for an amount exceeding the principal balance of your current mortgage and receive that increase in cash.

- *Equity in other real estate, such as a vacation home or rental property.* The same possibilities exist here as for your residence (second mortgage or refinance).

- *Other things you own, such as automobiles, trucks, recreational vehicles, boats, airplanes, and so on.* Unlike real estate, these items tend to decrease in value as time moves on, so their value to a lender and as collateral is significantly less than real estate. Also, it would be very unusual to find a lender who would take a second position (like a second mortgage) on these types of assets. In other words, if you already owe money on those items, they are not suitable collateral.

- *Life insurance policies.* If they have cash value, it is possible to borrow that amount of cash from the insurance company at a very low interest rate. (If your policies are strictly term life insurance, there is no cash value, and therefore they are not a source of funds that can be borrowed.)

Obtaining Money from Commercial Banks

The old saying goes that banks loan money only to people who do not need it. That implies that if you are trying to buy a business with other people's money, you don't have much money yourself, and therefore the bank will not lend money to you. That is partly true and partly an urban legend. Banks do loan money to people who need it. If they didn't, where would they find customers who borrow significant sums of money and, by paying interest to the bank, make the bank owners rich?

Plan Ahead

If you think you may need to borrow personal funds in order to buy a business or to provide working capital, make the arrangements and borrow the money *before* you quit your day job. Financial institutions like to loan money to people who are employed in a steady job, since they are most likely to make payments on time. Consumer loan departments are nervous about self-employed people and downright hyper about those who are just entering the self-employed population. Therefore, it's best to make loan arrangements while you are still casually looking for a business. In other words, borrow the funds when there is not yet any moral implication that you should disclose your goal of entrepreneurship. (Invest those borrowed funds in U.S. Treasury notes or other low-risk investments, and do not touch that money until you have exhausted all sources of other people's money.)

However, if you just stride into the bank lobby, sit at some loan officer's desk, and tell him or her that you would like to purchase Aunt Polly's Pancake House, a floundering operation next to the parole office, you can expect to be turned down. This is even more true if you have absolutely no restaurant experience and no experience hiring, firing, and supervising employees. The factors that could change the bank's answer from a "no" to a "yes" deserve attention.

Perhaps you have the training, the experience, and the smarts that you thought would appeal to a commercial bank. However, when you found a business for sale for $200,000, you dutifully applied to the bank for a $200,000 loan. The only collateral you could offer was the business itself, which was not in great condition. (That's why it was for sale.) The loan officer declined your deal but was polite as she ushered you out the door.

Were you disappointed? Of course. But look at it from the bank's viewpoint. If you did not make a go of the business, the bank would be left with the task of trying to liquidate the business to recover the money it loaned to you, and there is little chance that the equipment and inventory in the business would bring anything near $200,000 in a liquidation auction.

Now let's change the scene. Rather than immediately heading for the bank for the cash, make an offer for the business structured as 10 percent ($20,000) in cash and the balance of $180,000 payable in installments over the next five years. Now, when you approach the bank, your deal looks like this: the bank is loaning $20,000, secured by equipment inventory and other assets of the business that are easily worth $40,000, even in a liquidation sale. The bank, of course, is taking less risk for this $20,000 loan than would be in the case of a $200,000 loan when the same collateral is involved. A better deal for the bank means that approval for the loan is far more likely.

In other words, try first for the 100 percent owner financing when you buy a business. If the seller of the business insists on some cash up front, you can then go to the bank with a far more attractive deal for their part.

Choose a Bank That Is Small-Business Oriented

Many banks cater to the retail trade, specializing in such products as automotive loans, home equity lines of credit, financing appliance purchases, and so on. Other banks seem to want only well-heeled individuals, and a few banks do specialize in small-business needs. How do you know which is which? For starters, look at the bank's advertising, and check out its Web site. This should give you a clue as to what sort of clientele the bank is seeking. Banks seeking the retail customer generally have many branch locations plus additional ATM locations in grocery stores and similar places. Banks that cater to small businesses are quite often locally owned with no branches, or just a few. They quite often call themselves community banks.

Have the Requisite Experience

If you want financing for a pancake restaurant, either you, or a partner, should have management experience with a similar restaurant operation. Also, if you have experience operating a successful small business, that's a plus. It makes your experience far more appealing. Working for a large restaurant chain and following the corporate manual provides only minimum opportunity for creative management. Compare that to a small business in which the management manual, if there is one, is amended daily to meet changing competitive situations.

If you are buying a computer maintenance and repair business, or any technical service, the requirement for valid in-depth experience in that or a similar service is obvious.

If the seller of the business has been reasonably successful (the sale is not a distress sale) and agrees to stay on as an active consultant, you have a partial answer for questions about gaps in your own experience.

Buy a Business That Has Loyal Customers or Clients

If repeat business is almost guaranteed by the nature of the business, the probability that you will be able to repay bank financing is greatly enhanced. Businesses that fall into this category include insurance agencies, accounting firms, medical and dental practices, and similar entities.

Buy a Business That Is in the Right Location

For some businesses, such as retail stores and similar enterprises, success is all about location, location, location. Availability of parking and even the side of the street can be important. For other businesses, such as technical repair, location is less critical. However, the business should be in an area where the market is growing.

Prepare Projections of Income and Expenses of the Business

I do not know of any bank or other source of business financing that will even consider an application for business financing that does not include a projection of the expected income and expenses. The fact that you are buying a business rather than starting a business from scratch makes the preparation of projections a little easier, since your starting point is not a blank piece of paper but the financial and operating reports of the present owner of the business. Note that I say "starting point," because those reports of the present owner should be viewed with some reservations. Not all small-business owners keep accurate records, with the result that the operating reports may not be accurate.

As we are all aware, many business owners try to fudge the books with the intent of paying less income tax.

This distortion of the truth about operations is generally foolish. Not only do such business owners risk severe penalties from the IRS, but they pay the piper when it comes time to sell the business and retire. Those tax returns that understated the earnings from the business by a substantial percentage make the business appear far less valuable than it is. If you run into this situation, the seller will want you to base the price for the business on what he claims are the "real" profits. However, he may be just talking to try to increase the justifiable price of the business. Do not be misled by this. Base the offer on the hard facts, such as bank deposits, and if that offer is unacceptable to the seller, walk away.

Your Presentation to the Bank

No matter whom you talk to at the bank, whether it be the newly hired loan officer or, preferably, the president of the bank, remember that for business loans no one individual makes the decision. If you sell your contact at the bank on your business proposal, that contact has to sell your deal to the loan committee. Although an enthusiastic spiel may impress the bank contact, he or she will not be able to duplicate your verbal presentation in front of the loan committee. Therefore, you must provide that contact with written material that documents why, under your leadership, the business you are buying will thrive and be a profitable customer of the bank. That material, generally called a *business plan*, is discussed in Appendix A.

When the banker approves your loan, he or she undoubtebly will insist on a lien on all of the business assets, including equipment, inventory, and accounts receivable (if any). For that reason, you should not promise the seller of the business a lien on those assets, since the bank will insist on that collateral. However, if the seller insists on a lien on the business and equipment for his or her owner financing, go ahead and agree to it. Then, when the bank insists on that lien, tell the seller that you have the cash for him almost in hand, but he will have to subordinate his lien to that of the bank. Well, you know what happens when people see a bunch of money almost in hand and all they have to do to get it is sign one more piece of paper. In other words, you probably now own the business.

> To illustrate, Beatrice wanted to buy Sidney's hardware store. The agreed price for the business and the inventory was $500,000. Beatrice was able to convince Sidney to accept $50,000 in cash and future payments totaling $450,000 (plus interest), but Sidney insisted that the money owed him would be secured by a first lien on the inventory and store fixtures.

> Beatrice then applied to her local bank for a $50,000 loan which would be paid off within five years. The bank agreed to make the loan, but only if it could have the first position on the fixtures and inventory. That is, if the hardware store failed and Beatrice could not make the payments to the bank, the bank could repossess all of the inventory and fixtures and sell them, with the hope that the proceeds would pay the balance due on the $50,000 loan. Beatrice showed Sidney the bank's approval notice with the clause about having first lien rights, and Sidney objected and refused to relinquish his first lien position. However, Sidney waited for a couple of days and thought

about the $50,000 cash and the probable future payments of $450,000 to finance a comfortable retirement. The alternative was to continue looking for a buyer and continue to work until some unknown future date. Three days later, he relented and agreed to subordinate his claim on the fixtures and inventory to a lien to be held by the bank.

Beatrice now owned the hardware store.

Loans from Suppliers

Do not overlook companies that sell merchandise or supplies to the business you are buying. While it is highly unlikely that one supplier would be a source for funds sufficient to buy the business, small loans from several suppliers might go a long way toward swinging the deal. One of the most prevalent arrangements is not even called a loan, although, in essence, it is. A supplier might agree to sell you a large order of merchandise for the shelves that have been depleted by the seller of the business. In order to encourage you to buy from the supplier company, it would offer you extended terms for the large order. For instance, it might ship you the order with terms that you pay for the order over several months, or the terms might even delay any payment for at least 90 days. Obviously, when you're using borrowed funds to purchase a business, you need payment terms that extend over several years rather than months. However, this short-term financing from suppliers can be a big help in stocking shelves with merchandise and supplies.

Steve had operated a successful bakery in an upscale shopping center for several years. Now he was ready to retire, so he advertised his business for sale. When it became well known that the bakery was for sale, business began to fall off. Steve therefore reduced the amount of flour, sugar, shortening, and other baking supplies that he kept on hand. When Barbara showed up as a potential buyer, Steve was anxious to make some kind of deal and capture some of the value out of his business, rather than just close the door in the near future. Barbara had little money, but since she was experienced in retail store management and loved to bake pies, cakes, and bread, he agreed to her offer to purchase the business in installments. However, he was unwilling to advance any funds with which she could stock up on the necessary supplies. Barbara, being resourceful, contacted Fred's Finer Flour Company, which was Steve's principal supplier. Since Fred wished to continue this customer relationship, Fred's Finer Flour Company agreed to ship a large order of flour, sugar, and shortening, with one-sixth of that invoice being due in six monthly installments.

Did this arrangement work? Well, this episode happened well before the Atkins and South Beach diets hit the headlines, so Barbara prospered and paid off Steve and Fred. Note that it all happened because she used their money.

Will suppliers make similar arrangements for you? Just like banks and present owners of a business for sale, suppliers want to feel reasonably certain that you will succeed and be able to pay off the funds represented by the advances of merchandise and supplies. In other words, they too will want to know about your experience and your business success stories. Provide them with the same background material that you created for the bank and the business seller.

The Shortcut—Buy Out Your Boss Using His or Her Money

This is the ultimate deal for buying a business with other people's money. If you are working for a small business and the owner has reached a reasonable retirement age, it's time to make a pitch to the boss. Who better knows your capabilities as far as managing the business, your integrity, and your ability to deal successfully with customers and employees? Assuming your boss rates you highly, you would be the number-one choice among prospective buyers, with the possible exception of someone who could pay the price in cash, which we know is very unlikely. Also, selling the business to you would be transparent to customers. In other words, it would appear to customers that Mr. Boss had retired and you are now the general manager. Everything else in the relationship of the customers with your business remains the same. As for suppliers, they need to know a little more, such as who is ultimately responsible for the payment of the business's debts. This can be handled privately, without publicity, so there is no apprehension among your customers.

The sticking point, of course, is determining what you should pay (in installments) for the business. To you, the business is more valuable than it is to any other prospective buyer, since there is no learning process for you, while any other buyer has to learn the ins and outs of your company and, most importantly, develop a relationship with major customers. Unfortunately, Mr. Boss has figured that out and will demand a high price—as much as he can get. (Hasn't he always underpaid you?) What this means is that this is not a deal you can automatically slip into. Just as with buying any business, you need to do your homework by creating a business plan that determines whether or not you can succeed if you pay the high price your boss demands.

Buy a Franchise, but Not with the Franchisor's Money

When a small business is eminently successful, the owner will often become a franchisor and set up a network of franchised locations throughout the country and the world. You can enter the business world by buying one of those franchised locations, erecting a building according to the franchisor's specifications, and operating a business therein. Buying such a franchise has its advantages and disadvantages. Among the advantages are that you benefit from national advertising, operations procedures which have already been developed and debugged, and other assistance that is available. Among the disadvantages are that, although the franchise store will arrange for financing of the building and much of the equipment, it will insist on a substantial upfront cash payment. That's because the franchisor has certain upfront costs, such as the commission paid to the franchisor's sales person. If you buy a currently operating franchise from its owner, then you may be able to negotiate owner financing as you could with any business. However, in buying a used franchise, take care that you meet the approval of the franchisor and that there is an adequate time left before the franchise agreement expires and comes up for renewal. (At renewal time, you may find the franchisor's current terms may make renewal on your part unattractive, or the franchisor may opt not to renew the franchise.)

Friends and Relatives as a Source of Borrowed Funds

This is probably the most unattractive source of funds, although it is often used. What makes it unattractive? The fact that the histories of small business are littered with episodes of families torn apart by business loans to relatives that were never paid back. Business associates are just that—people you associate with for business reasons. When those business reasons no longer exist, you go your separate ways, and if one of you is a bad debt of the other, so be it. Your family and close personal friends are for life. My recommendation is to keep it that way by not borrowing substantial amounts from them.

If you do insist on so borrowing, make sure they understand that they are entering a business relationship and that they understand the risks that they are taking. There should be no question about it being essential that any business deal with a close friend or relative be in writing. Obviously, at all costs avoid borrowing from the young or the very old who are least able to understand the risks involved.

The Government—the Small Business Administration (SBA)

I have left the discussion of this source until last because it is the least understood and the most complex to use. And there are reasons for the complexity: Periodically, the Congress tinkers with the law under which the SBA operates, and the SBA tinkers with the rules and the myriad forms that are generated by any government agency.

The first eye-opener about the SBA is that it does not currently make loans directly to small businesses, although it used to do that some years ago. What it does do is work with commercial banks and other lenders so that the bank is actually lending the money to the small business and the SBA is guaranteeing 75 percent of the loan. That is, if you default on an

SBA-guaranteed loan of $100,000, the SBA will reimburse the bank $75,000 of that loss, so the bank loses only $25,000.

The usual procedure to apply for an SBA-guaranteed loan looks something like this:

- You apply to the bank for the funds with which to buy the business, just as we discussed under the heading of commercial banks. You would submit a business plan, complete with projections, as well as a resume of your experience, education, and success stories.

- The bank will evaluate you and your application, and make one of three decisions. One, it will decide you're a hopeless dreamer without funds and send you on your way. Or, two, it will decide that you are well experienced in successfully operating other small businesses, have some personal assets that will serve as collateral, and that the probability of your success is so high it will loan you the funds with which to purchase a business. Or, three, it will make the decision (which it frequently makes) to determine that the probability of your success is above average but not strong enough for the bank to take all the risk by itself. In that case, you will hear the dreaded words that "your loan is approved if you can secure an SBA guarantee." That process involves several government forms, and if you are like me, you have never seen a simple government form. If the bank is experienced in submitting SBA applications, it can give you some help and encouragement in completing the forms. However, because part of those forms consists of financial information, you may need to spend a few dollars for professional accounting help.

- You then submit these forms to the bank, and they submit them to the SBA.

- After what seems like an interminable period of time, the SBA may commit to the guarantee. Of course, by that time the business you anticipated purchasing may have been sold to someone else. That's discouraging, but now the SBA has its information on your background and other material. For the next business you find, you'll only have to update the financial information for this business and, hopefully, secure the loan guarantee in time to use it.

If you prefer, you can approach the SBA first and seek its approval before you approach the bank. However, this leaves you without a bank resource to assist you in completing all the forms, so your need for professional advice from an accountant will increase.

To Summarize

Yes, you can buy a business without using your own cash. Negotiate with the seller of the business so that you pay the bulk of the price in installments over future years. If the seller will not budge from a demand for some cash, take the time to prepare a business plan and look for help from your local bank or other lender.

CHAPTER 4

Do You Want Partners?

In this chapter, we use the term "partners" to mean anyone who is a co-owner of your business, regardless of whether it is structured as a corporation or other business form. In other words, using the term "partners" when the business is formed as a corporation is technically incorrect, but I will cover that technicality later. This chapter is devoted to a discussion of whether you need partners (and their money) and if so, who they should be.

Why You Might Have One or More Partners

There are probably as many reasons to have a partner as there are partnerships in the country. However, most reasons fall into one of these categories:

- The partner is a source of funds with which to buy and/or operate the business.

- The partner has expertise that you lack.

- The partner has many business and/or political contacts that are helpful in winning contracts and promoting the business.

- The partner's personality complements yours.

- The partner is much younger than you, facilitating your retirement some day.

- The partner is the older seller of this business, which enables you to buy a business.

- You and your spouse started a part-time business in your garage, which has now grown to a full-time downtown business.

- The new partner is your down-and-out brother-in-law who needs a job with some prestige.

- The partner is your high school buddy or college roommate.

What follows is a discussion of some of these possibilities.

The Partner Has Money

You have found the perfect business for sale. You have worked in that industry and have the management and sales experience that makes your success almost a 100 percent probability. Everything is working in your favor, except that the seller demands an immediate partial payment of $50,000 in cash only. Where can you find the cash you so desperately need? You mention this to your barber, and he responds by saying that he knows a man who knows a woman who recently inherited a substantial estate and is looking for investments where she can get an exceptionally high return.

You follow up on the lead and find this situation: Denise, this wealthy lady, not only wants a high-return investment but she wants to be part of the action. She wants to be involved to the point that she knows her investment is being handled wisely and will not be frittered away by poor management or inattention. In other words, she wants a significant say in the management, and if profits or the cash balance start to slide downhill, she wants to be the top management. To ensure that she has that option when she advances the funds, she wants to have 60 percent of the partnership while you have 40 percent. Should you accept this arrangement in order to buy this dream business? It means that you would be a junior partner, so without an agreement to the contrary, she would make the final decisions on any questions of management policy. In day-to-day operations, you would be little more than an employee with an equity interest, which means you would get to share 40 percent of the profits of the business. Whether or not those profits are paid out of cash would be at the discretion of the senior partner, so if Denise doesn't need the money, she may decide that the profits should not be distributed to the partners (you and her) but kept in the business to finance expansion. That puts you in the same position you were when you first found this business opportunity—you have no money!

It might look as though this is a deal you should pass up. But before you make that decision, be aware that what I outlined here is a synopsis of which you might call the default way the partnership laws specify. However, an agreement among all of the partners in an enterprise takes precedence over the law. In other words, you can be creative in developing other arrangements that would satisfy Denise. For instance, you could offer her this structure:

- Denise invests the needed $50,000 in the partnership.
- In exchange, she receives a $40,000 note from the partnership, paying her a return of 10 percent ($4,000 per year). For the other

$10,000, she receives a 40-percent interest in the partnership and would receive 40 percent of the profits.

- As general manager, you would receive a specific salary for your labor. (Both your salary and the interest paid to Denise would be deducted from profits before computing the 40-60 split.)

- To allay her fears that you might mismanage, the agreement could also state that if the partnership is more than 30 days late with an interest payment due to Denise, she will be entitled to take over general management of the business. As there is, of course, some possibility that this might happen, you also need to resolve whether you and Denise are compatible and can compromise where differences of opinion arise. Spending some time discussing your respective business philosophies can be helpful, as can discussions with mutual friends and acquaintances. You can also try questioning her employer or former employers, but in today's litigious society, most employers are reluctant to discuss present or past employees.

There are many modifications you can make to a partnership arrangement such as this. They are limited only by the creativity of the partners and their lawyers. When trying to put together a partnership agreement, keep the goals of each prospective partner in mind.

- Those of us who have little or no money are looking for an opportunity to generate substantially more cash than we need for basic living. To that end, we want the opportunity to run a business efficiently and promote it effectively rather than as our present boss thinks a business should be run.

- The partners making a cash investment want some assurance that their investment will be kept whole and that it will earn a return at a reasonable rate for the level of risk involved in the business. Also, they hope for a windfall when your business turns out to be another Microsoft or Intel.

- The partners who will work in the business, providing sweat equity, do not want to give away a large hunk of the business in return for an investment by a passive investor.

Are these conflicting interests? You bet they are, but running a business is full of compromises. You compromise with customers on prices and payment terms, you compromise on the flip side of that with suppliers, you compromise with employees as to work hours and rate of pay. You might as well practice the strategies of compromise with your prospective partner.

The Partner Has Expertise That You Lack

If you always wanted to own a hardware store, but have never worked in one, you may be a little nervous about contracting to buy one that's for sale. And if you're nervous, the bank also would be nervous. You can overcome that nervousness by joining forces with a partner who has had years of experience in the hardware and related businesses, such as construction. That could make your proposal to the seller of the business, the bank, or any other money source far more attractive.

The Partner Has Contacts

Contacts with important individuals has made many a business. This is particularly true in doing business with large corporations or governments.

Although the awarding of contracts should be based on merit, knowing where the door to that contracting office is, and finding a welcome mat out, is a big help in winning profitable contracts.

The Partner's Personality Complements Yours

The graveyard of businesses is well populated by promising young enterprises that failed simply because the top management either did not understand the importance of financial controls and planning or was incapable of performing the detailed tasks inherent in that planning.

> Joe Woodworker was a skilled artisan who operated a waterfront boat repair facility. While his services were much in demand and he was always busy, he never seemed to have any money. He tried to solve that problem by hiring skilled helpers, but the cash drain seemed to get even larger, and eventually led to bankruptcy. The problem was that Joe charged his customers an hourly rate for work performed, but keeping track of those hours and those of his employees was not in Joe's skill set. He often forgot to keep track of his time, and it was not unusual to misplace the time records that his employees submitted. The result was that he often collected just enough money on a job to pay the wages of his employees. There was nothing to cover overhead and profit.

> Joe was not blind to this problem. He actually tried to take care of it by hiring Archie, a freelance bookkeeper, to come in once a week and prepare customer invoices, keep the checkbook reasonably organized, and write payroll checks. However, this did not answer the problem of adequate timekeeping, nor did Archie do any cash-flow planning or other management tasks. He did the minimum that Joe paid him to do

and left. In other words, Joe needed an executive, a CFO if you will, who would have the interests of the business at heart. However, CFOs are expensive and beyond the reach of small businesses like Joe's. Joe did without, and struggled for survival over several years until he fell into the clutches of the bankruptcy court.

If you are like Joe—a heavyweight in the marketing or production areas but not so good with the details—a details-oriented partner could be the solution. As such, a partner will expect to share in the increasing profits as a business grows; he or she may also join you in living on a subsistence wage until the business growth justifies substantial executive salaries and benefits. Be aware that burnout is a malady afflicting many CPAs in public practice. I have seen several instances where entrepreneurs have enticed one of the skilled but burned-out people to join them in an enterprise as a partner. The results have been excellent.

The Seller of the Business Can Be Your Temporary Partner

In the process of buying a business, you could set up a short-term (a period of years) partnership. As that period passes, the partnership would make substantially higher payments to the seller/partner than to you, but a big part of those payments would be for the purchase of the business. The advantage of this arrangement is that the seller is assured that he will have access to the accounting books and also be able to head off any mistakes you might be about to make. (Presumably, he has already suffered from the results of those mistakes.) The advantage to you is that the arrangement enables you to buy the business. The disadvantage, of course, is the disadvantage of all partnerships—the difficulty of getting along on a day-to-day basis.

This arrangement requires a very carefully drawn partnership agreement. Be sure to clarify the allocation between what money is for the purchase of the business and what money is partners' salary and share of the current profits. How that allocation is set up can have significant tax consequences, so be sure that the attorney who draws up the agreement is well-versed in tax law.

The Part-Time Family Business Has Grown Up

You or your spouse started a part-time business in the garage or the spare bedroom. As it grew, your spouse became involved, you both quit your day jobs, you rented commercial space, and the world looks good. If yours is not the first marriage of both of you and there are children and stepchildren involved, think seriously about whose business this is. Is it yours? Is it your spouse's? Has one of you essentially given half of the business to the other, making it a partnership? Who will inherit the business? Obviously, it's high time to resolve those questions and draw up wills and estate plans that document your decisions.

Your Down-and-Out Relative Needs a Job

You might do this under pressure from other relatives, but no matter how much pressure they apply, don't give in. If you must, you can give such an individual a job, but not a partnership interest. You can fire an employee, but getting rid of a partner can be a very expensive process. In other words, do not make your relative a partner.

You Want to Include Your Best Friend in Your Deal

This always seems like the perfect partnership. You know you're compatible with each other from time spent in ball games, sports bars, camping trips, and so on. But the problem is that you probably do not complement each other. You are both Type As or you are both Type Bs. You will argue over details of a sales presentation or the maintenance schedule of a piece of equipment while the bills pile up and taxes remain unpaid, or vice versa. If this does not describe the two of you, then perhaps you do complement each other and would work well in a partnership. Be forewarned, though, that many long-term friendships often come apart because they also became business relationships.

People Who May Help You Find Potential Partners

The most sought-after partners, and probably the most difficult to find, are those who can invest the dollars to make the purchase of a business happen. The basic tactic is to talk to people—everyone you know or don't know. You never know who among friends or strangers has a rich Uncle Harry who is looking to invest in the same type of business you're considering. (Of course, if the recipient of your conversation is also thinking of buying a business, he may not refer you to his Uncle Harry, preferring to keep that possible source of financing for himself.)

Here is a short list of possible referral sources of prospective investors that should start your creative juices flowing:

- Accountants, such as CPAs and tax preparers, are in an enviable position, in that they know who actually has money and who has to scrimp every month to make the lease payment on the BMW. As you must be aware, accountants in general are a fiscally conservative lot, so selling them on your prospective enterprise will take effort, including the presentation of a business plan in projections as discussed in Chapter 3. Of course, if you do not sell the accountant, she may still put you in contact with an investor, but the chances of that individual becoming your investor/partner are remote if his accountant has a low opinion of your prospective enterprise.

- Financial planners are often lumped in with accountants, but many of them will be unproductive sources because they make their living from the commissions they are paid to sell their clients' mutual funds, stocks, annuities, and bonds. Other financial planners generate their income by charging their clients fees and passing the commissions they earn on to the client. They are known as *fee only* financial planners. Since they have no incentive to earn commissions, they will evaluate your proposition and pass it along to their clients if they agree that yours is a viable investment opportunity.

- Just like accountants, lawyers who handle corporate affairs and deal in wills and estate planning also know who has investment funds and who doesn't.

- Commercial bankers can be a source of referrals to investors. Although they have interest-bearing products to sell to wealthy customers, some of their customers specifically want equity investments where they can accept the risk and may earn greater returns. Bear in mind that large banks usually have financial planning and stock brokerage operations, so the previous discussion about financial planners may apply. For that reason, I would start checking with the local community banks.

- Vendors who sell to the industry in which you are interested can be a great source of knowledge. They know who is buying lots of supplies and equipment as well as those who are paying or not paying for those items. Talk to both the sales manager and the credit manager of companies that supply your industry.

- Franchisors know which franchisees are operating profitably and which ones have hit upon hard times and are for sale as a going business. Try to determine if the franchise location is in trouble because of location or if it's something such as owner illness which can be easily overcome—by you as a healthy new owner. (Remember that buying an operating franchise probably means that you will have to move to a different part of the country.)

- Business or economic development offices: These usually operate as quasi-government offices, or under the auspices of an educational organization, with the mission of attracting businesses to locate in the area of the city, metropolitan area, or state that funds the development office. While these organizations generally make it into the headlines when they land a large employer to locate in the supported area, they usually will aid small enterprises which add activity to the local economy. It's worth a visit to a development office. The staff may know of someone who might be an angel. Some of these organizations may maintain a database of possible investors in the state or local area.

There is one database of both investors and investment opportunities that covers the entire nation. Known as *Active Capital*, it is a system for matching small businesses in need of capital with financial angels who bestow money on small businesses. (If your Uncle Ulysses no longer wants to be your financial resource, you might find his replacement at Active Capital.)

Well, "bestow" may not be a good choice of words, for it implies a grant or gift, and financial angels are not in the business of "giving." Just like any source of capital, they expect a return on their money. The term "angel" describes wealthy individuals who not only invest in but take a direct interest in the fortunes of the business they finance. For that reason, they invest in just one or a very few small businesses. They differ from venture capital firms, which pool the investment money of several individuals and/or institutions so that the risk is spread out over many entities. An angel, on the other hand, has all of his or her eggs in one or a few baskets, which might infer that their risk is greater. However, their ability to be directly involved in the business they are financing somewhat offsets that risk. Indeed, these angels are quite often entrepreneurs who have "made it," sold their business, and seek an opportunity to be still involved in the challenge of the business world.

The concept of Active Capital is an idea that was hatched by the Small Business Administration. While the concept was admirable, there was little growth in the database. It has now been spun off into a separate nonprofit organization. The new management is composed of individuals who are committed to the success of the operation. While it is still in the development mode, it would be worth your time to check it out if you have a well thought-out business plan for the business you propose to acquire. The information as to limits on the size of the enterprise that can be listed on the database and other details, as well as contact information, are in Appendix C.

Will you be able to attract a financial angel? You may be able to if you have a well thought-out and documented business plan, knowledge of the industry, and experience in management. Are you opening another neighborhood hardware store? If your business plan reflects that this will be just another small cookie-cutter hardware store, your chances of finding an angel are probably slim. On the other hand, if you are incorporating a new marketing gimmick in your hardware store plans, and that gimmick promises to propel you into becoming a sizable competitor to Home Depot and Lowe's, you may pique the interest of an angel who would like to be part of that scene. Look for your angel.

Stay Out of Trouble with the Government(s)

It's important to remember that if you seek financing from anyone other than your Aunt Alice, an old friend, a wealthy individual, or a commercial bank or similar institution, and that money source is a passive investor with no management responsibilities, you have to be concerned with the securities laws and regulations in the 50 states and the federal government, by way of the Securities and Exchange Commission. In other words, if you have a hot idea that will attract a some "average-Joe" investors, you will want to facilitate their flow of investment money to you by incorporating your business and selling your corporation's stock to these enthusiastic investors. So, you will have to put up with the hassle of government regulators and their paperwork. Read "government" as not only the federal Securities and Exchange Commission, but also some or all of the 50 states and the District of Columbia. But it's not all bad. The SEC has special simplified procedures for entrepreneurs who are raising $5 million or less, while many of the states have standardized their registration procedures. The aforementioned Active Capital offers help in the area of stock and other security registration in addition to its matching service. In the process of discussing Active Capital with Phil Borden, its CEO, he wrote me an e-mail in which he described the area of security regulation for small business better, I think, than I could. Here is his e-mail:

"The SEC is only one regulatory entity overseeing the registration of private offers. Perhaps more important are the state securities regulators. They can overrule the SEC on some regulatory issues. Every state has its own securities regulations. When ACE-Net first began, its originators realized the potential mess this would create for a national organization, so it pressed to harmonize those regulations. The result was the Model Accredited Investors Exemption (MAIE). It sets up a standard for all state regulatory bodies.

"12 states accept MAIE regulations word for word. 36 other states and territories accept the MAIE with modifications. A couple of states, like California and New York and Texas, make major changes. Policy for all state regulators is set by the North American Securities Administrators Association (NASAA). They track and publish all the state regulatory information as well as recommending changes from time to time as business practices change. They love the MAIE, because it makes their job easier. They regularly cite ACE-Net/Active Capital as a key benefit for small business because it creates 'legal deals' consistent with NASAA policies.

"NASAA accepts the 'U-7' as an offering document adequate to register offerings in all states. This form is a detailed application, kind of like a financially oriented business plan on steroids. It has 110 or so questions, etc. It is not necessary to fill out a U-7 form, but doing so guarantees the entrepreneur who fills it out will meet all state regulatory requirements.

"Active Capital is the only organization offering the kind of listing/matching service you write about through which an entrepreneur can both create a business plan for others to look at and get registered at the same time. That is, it creates both an offering document and a registration document. The folks on the Internet that offer entrepreneurs the chance to get their business plans seen without registration advice, especially when they are showing those plans in multiple states, may in fact be exposing the entrepreneur to serious consequences; that is because entrepreneurs cannot engage in 'general solicitation' unless they either are registered under one of several particular regulations or made exempt by them. By the way, there is a way to get entirely around state regulations, but it requires an SB-2 form that makes the U-7 look like a Dr. Seuss book, plus steep legal fees.

"There are other sites offering more direct matching, or the opportunity for an entrepreneur to get a business plan before an angel. However, they often do not themselves understand how costly what they are doing may be to the entrepreneur downstream. The SEC or state regulators are not going to get bent about a $10,000 or even several hundred thousand dollar equity raise. But if the company continues to grow and needs more investment (and this typically is the case), an early 'illegal' raise could poison that deal. An example known to almost everyone is Google. Their initial public offering was held up 3–4 months because they had innocently implemented an 'illegal' employee stock plan that poisoned their IPO. They were able to clean it up relatively easily for a number of reasons. But the fact is that a company that runs afoul of these stock offering regulations must offer the right of rescission to every investor, alive or dead. Not typically easy.

"Finally, I'd like to clear up something you glossed over, but probably covered earlier in your ms—the Uncle Julius example. You do not need to register stock for sale privately so long as the persons you are selling it to are known to you beforehand—i.e., you have a prior relationship. Registration rules only kick in when you are offering to sell to people with whom you are not in a prior relationship. And, a critical distinction at this juncture is whether or not the investor is an 'accredited investor.' There is a definition you easily can find online, but it boils down to whether or not the investor can afford to lose the investment. Regulators like to insure investors are accredited because it makes them comfortable that the entrepreneur or his representative or agent is not fooling the little old lady in tennis shoes."

In Appendix B, you will find more information in the form of a "question and answer" document from the SEC, a "frequently asked questions" page from the Internet site of Active Capital, and a list of state securities regulators. Incidentally, I have no financial interest in Active Capital.

Keep in mind that many referral sources need to be sold on your plans to purchase an enterprise before they will suggest your proposition to their client. So, have your plans well organized in your head. It helps to have a short summary (no more than two pages) plus a copy of your full-blown business plan with you when you meet with a referral prospect. Leave at least the summary with everyone you talk to, and leave the plan with those who show interest. (If you have a unique idea, particularly a technical improvement in a product or process, you should get a nondisclosure agreement from anyone who receives a copy of your business plan. Have your lawyer draw one up for you.)

Companies in the Business of Being a Partner

There are two classes of firms that make a business of becoming a partner in an up-and-coming enterprise. Both types have requirements as to what sort of enterprise they will fund, so read on to see if you might qualify.

Venture Capitalist

A venture capital firm could be your partner. These capital-supplying firms are generally pools of investors (both individuals and institutions) who invest by taking equity positions in small and medium businesses. That is, they want to be not only an investor, but also a partner, and to have a hand in strategic decisions of management. As to their goals, the National Venture Capital Association states that a venture capital firm "invests in companies that represent the opportunity for a high rate of return within five to seven years." This does not rule out venture capital financing if you are buying an existing business, for you would fit into a classification the Association calls "expansion stage financing." However, the business would have to be at a point in its development where additional financing would enable it to take off and grow very rapidly. Because of this rather restrictive requirement that growth happen quickly and soon, only a very small percentage of proposals that venture capitalists receive are ever funded by them. However, if you think you might have a chance with them, there is more information at the Association's Web site, http://www.nvca.org. It includes instructions on how to obtain a directory of member venture capital firms.

Small Business Investment Company (SBIC)

Funding by an SBIC is always a possibility, although one of the requirements seems to be that you can handle filling in obtuse government forms. An SBIC is essentially a venture capital firm that works under the umbrella of the SBA. It is initially funded by private money from individuals and private institutions, and that capital is augmented by substantial funds from the SBA. This arrangement was created by Congress years ago and does have some requirements for favoring minorities, females, and businesses in low-income areas. If you fit one of those favored groups, your chances of being able to secure equity financing from an SBIC are good. ("Equity financing" translates as "you have a partner who will be expecting frequent reports from you and will also provide advice as to improvements you can make in your operation." Those report requirements from this partner are part of the price you pay for the financing.) If you are successful in securing financing from an SBIC, you may find that part of the financing is through buying equity in your business and part will be a direct loan. (The loan is from the SBIC, not the SBA.) You can find more details on the SBA's Web site, http://www.sba.gov/INV/forentre.html.

The Form That Your Partnership Should Use

In the course of negotiating for the business you buy, you will be able to find out whether it is running as a sole proprietorship, partnership, C corporation, S corporation, or limited liability company (LLC). There is no law that says you have to continue the business in the same legal form. For instance, if the business is operating as a partnership and you believe you would be better off operating as an S corporation, the time to make that change is when you buy the business. Accounting trauma is brought on by changes in the legal form of conducting business as well as by change of ownership, so you can save professional fees by lumping both traumas together. Be sure you obtain competent legal and accounting advice in this area. That sounds expensive, and it can be. But you can cut down on the hours (and fees) spent in conversation with these professionals by preparing yourself by some reading. (See my recommendations at the end of this chapter.) Among the factors to be considered are these:

- *Protection of assets.* I think we all are aware that if we pour our hard-earned money into the business and the business slides down the tubes, we have lost that money. What is a real blow is if we find that we have not only lost the money invested in the business, but we have also lost our home, our boat, our airplane, and our valuable antiques.

- *Simplicity*. This is nearly a forgotten word in our complex society, but we can still aspire to it.

- *Flexibility*. If your agreement with other owners calls for some owners to receive a greater share of the profits, even though they own a smaller share of the business, you do need flexibility.

- *Ease of entry and exit*. If you and your partner agree to disagree and one of you wants out of the business, will the paperwork that documents the farewell be hassle free?

- *The tax effects of your choice of business form*. You don't want to put in long hours in your business and finally earn a much-above-average income only to have the tax man grab much of it.

The Business Form Choices

Here are the choices of business forms and how they stack up with regard to the four factors we listed:

GENERAL PARTNERSHIP

This is what you have if you and your buddy set up a Web site to sell round-bottom coffee cups. (It is impossible to set them down and work while you're enjoying your coffee break.) Because you did not generate any paper or file specific forms with your state government, you have a general partnership. This means that the personal assets of you and your buddy are all available to creditors of your business, without limit. So, if you do not pay the lady who owns the cup factory for the cups you had her make for you, she will soon be driving your Lexus.

A general partnership is relatively simple to set up and run, especially if each partner owns 50 percent of the business and 50 percent of the profits. As for flexibility, a general partnership has that attribute. All it takes is an agreement, preferably on paper, as to how ownership, profits, and losses are to be divided. If one partner is to receive more pay for his or her labor than does the other partner, that arrangement should be part of the partnership agreement.

If there are more than two partners, or if it is not a fifty-fifty partnership, the partnership agreement must specify how much of the partnership each partner owns. This can be specified as either a percentage or a fraction.

The income tax on the earnings of a partnership is handled this way. The taxable income of the partnership is divided between the partners in the same percentage as specified by the partnership agreement. Each partner adds his or her share of the taxable income on to other taxable income on their individual income tax return. Then they compute the tax on that total. This may result in one partner paying tax on his or her partnership income at a higher rate than does some other partner. (The first partner would have other income, such as interest income from investments.)

LIMITED LIABILITY COMPANY (LLC)

This is a business form that has newly arrived in the United States during the last 20 years. Basically, it is a general partnership to which a state has granted limited liability. That means that if you formed your coffee cup business as an LLC, the lady who owns a coffee cup factory might end up owning your business, but you would get to keep your Lexus. Note that while a general partnership can be set up with just a handshake in our verbal agreement, an LLC must be registered with the state in order to have the limited liability protection. The only other difference between an LLC and a general partnership is some terminology: While the owners of a general partnership are called *partners*, the owners of an LLC are called *members*.

As for the tax picture, unless an LLC chooses otherwise, it is taxed in the same manner as a general partnership. That is, the members pay individual tax on their share of the LLC income. (An LLC may choose to be taxed as a corporation if it files a specific form with the IRS. However, that defeats one of the usual reasons for doing business as an LLC, which is to have partnership taxation with limited liability.)

CORPORATION

This form of doing business has been around for centuries. Most of us are familiar with the term *corporation* or *incorporated*, since that is the form that nearly all large publicly owned businesses use. However, the corporate form is not limited to Microsoft and IBM, but can be used by the smallest of businesses, even that part-time business people run from their kitchen tables. At the small-business end of the spectrum, there's little difference from a partnership or LLC except for some formalities. Like the LLC, the corporation must be registered with one or more states and must issue shares of stock to its owners (called *stockholders*) in proportion to the ownership ratios that the owners agreed upon when dreaming up the business. Along with the LLC, the liability of stockholders for the corporation's debts is limited to only the investment the stockholders have made in the corporation. (If you use this form for your coffee cup business, you would also get to keep your Lexus.)

For income tax purposes only, there are two subdivisions of corporations. If the corporation does not file certain forms with the IRS, it is a regular corporation, known as a C corporation. As such, it pays income tax on its earnings and if it pays some of those earnings to the stockholders in the form of dividends, the stockholders pay tax on those dividends. (This is the famous "double taxation" of corporations.)

If the corporation files certain forms with the IRS, it may be able to gain status as an S corporation. If that is so, the income of the corporation is divided up proportionately among the stockholders, and the stockholders add it to their other income, such as wages, and pay tax on the total. In other words, the taxation of S corporation income is very similar to that of a partnership's.

WHAT IF YOU GO IT ALONE, WITHOUT A PARTNER?

If you have located a source that is loaning you the money with which to buy a business, you don't have to have a partner. You can go it alone. What sort of business form do you use then? You can operate as a sole proprietor. This has the advantage of simplicity, but it comes with unlimited liability for any business debts that you incur.

To avoid that unwanted feature, you can form a corporation and operate your business as a corporation in which you own all of the stock. That will require a little more care in your recordkeeping, and you will have another tax return that needs to be prepared every year for the corporation. Beyond that, the IRS will require that part of the money drawn out of the corporation be classified as wages. (The reason: The IRS wants you to pay Social Security tax on it.)

As an alternative, you generally can operate as a single-owner LLC. Because a business with one owner does not fit the definition of partnership, you cannot file a partnership income tax return. Instead, you are treated as a sole proprietor. Because this avoids the complication of keeping track of payroll taxes, you may find the LLC to be an advantage. However, if you elect corporation status, some of the money you take out of the corporation can be classified as distribution of profits rather than salary, and distribution of profits is not subject to Social Security tax.

More Information on Forms of Doing Business

I know, this subject can be pretty confusing when it's condensed into these few paragraphs. If you are up to digesting more information in this area, you could start with my book titled *Small Business Formation Handbook*, published by John Wiley & Sons, Inc. For more information on corporations, I have written *Incorporate Your Business*, also published by John Wiley & Sons, Inc.

CHAPTER 5

Technicalities of Buying a Business

Most readers will be familiar with the intricacies of buying a home, including the fact that you need to know what you are buying. For instance, do the draperies and carpet go with the house? (Back in the early part of the twentieth century modern plumbing was still a novelty, so some people viewed the plumbing fixtures as personal property that would be carried off by the seller. I understand it was common practice to include, in the sales contract, a list of the bathroom fixtures that would stay with the house.) Even more care is necessary to specify what you are buying when you make an offer for a business. What follows are various ways of structuring the purchase of a business with some thoughts as to their consequences.

Buy Just Certain Assets of the Business

This is the least risky way to buy a business because the sales agreement, or an addendum to it, should list the assets in detail. Doing it this way insures that if the seller owes any money to suppliers or other people, paying them is the seller's responsibility—not yours. If you are buying a sole proprietorship, be aware that the law regards the sole proprietor and the business to be one and the same, so you cannot buy any sole proprietorship, since that would amount to placing the sole proprietor in the role of your indentured servant, which has been illegal for some time. Therefore, buying the assets is the only way you can buy a business that is operated as a sole proprietor. These assets may consist of at least the following.

Cash

Obviously, it doesn't make sense to buy the cash that is in the cash drawer. You can buy your own cash at the bank.

Accounts Receivable from Customers

If possible, try to avoid tying up your money or your partner's money in this nonproductive asset. The exception is if you have been able to negotiate most of the total purchase price as seller financing, and the owner is willing to take payments for the accounts receivable over several years, just as he or she will accept installment payments for inventory and fixtures. This arrangement can be a good deal for your cash flow, since you should be able to collect most of the accounts receivable within 30 to 60 days and pay the seller for them over a period of years. Be sure to analyze the accounts receivable to make sure they are collectible, as covered in Chapter 2 under valuing assets.

Other Accounts Receivable

Generally, you should leave any miscellaneous receivables with the seller and let him or her collect them. The exception would be long-term employees who have received a small advance on next week's paycheck. Because a business already owes the employees money for days already worked, collection of the advance is pretty well assured.

Inventory

Watch out for obsolete inventory, as covered in Chapter 2. Do not include the old stuff in your offer unless you offer pennies on the dollar.

Equipment

It is a good idea to list every piece of equipment that has a value greater than $100 and to include the model number and serial number in an addendum to the sales agreement.

If your lawyer is worth her fee, she will check the public records at the courthouse for financing statements or other documents that indicate the equipment has been pledged to secure a bank loan or other debt. If that is the case, the seller will need to reduce the purchase price by the amount of the debt and pay off the debt at closing. If you have succeeded in arranging seller financing, simply deduct the amount of the debt secured by the equipment from the total payment you will make to the seller. Also, commercial banks are famous for securing a lien on all assets when they make a loan to a business. If your lawyer finds out that that is the case, be sure to reduce the present or future payments to the seller by the amount of the debt and pay off the debt yourself. Of course, that procedure should be part of the purchase agreement.

Bulk Sales Law

Most states have bulk sales laws, which exist to protect the creditors of the seller. Generally, such laws require that a notice be given to every creditor of the seller that materials, supplies, merchandise, or other inventory are being transferred in bulk to the buyer of the business. "Bulk transfer" is defined as a transfer in bulk and not in the course of ordinary business. The creditors can then make a claim against the assets being transferred. Obviously, this can create a problem if you are purchasing the business with 100 percent seller financing. If there is some cash (from a lender or partner) involved, that cash should be directed to the creditors who have filed a claim.

If procedures that are required under the bulk sales law are not carefully carried out, you could end up paying twice for the business's inventory. It goes without saying that you therefore need to involve your lawyer in making sure you properly comply with the law.

Assume the Liabilities of the Business When You Buy the Assets?

Obviously, if your agreement simply states that you assume the liabilities of the business, you could be opening a Pandora's box. As I mentioned before, a search of the public records should reveal debts that have been incurred in the normal course of acquiring assets or borrowing from a bank. However, what if the seller has very recently received a letter from an attorney advising the seller that the attorney's client has a major claim for injury while on the business's premises? If it develops that the court determines that the seller has to pay that claim, does that general assumption of liabilities include that claim? Because you don't want to spend time worrying about such matters in the future, be specific as to what liabilities you are assuming.

Again, it may be advantageous to assume certain liabilities of the seller as partial payment for the business. This is especially true if the liabilities consist of installments spread out over some future periods. This arrangement amounts to the holder of the installment note financing part of your purchase of the business for you.

In addition to the above, a competent lawyer will include an indemnification agreement or clause in the sales agreement by which the seller promises to reimburse the buyer for any undisclosed liabilities that arise in the future. However, if the seller decides to retire in Tasmania, that clause may be of little or no value.

The Seller Takes on Risks, Too

When you agree to pay the seller's liabilities, that does not release the seller from liability for payment of those debts if you fail to pay them. Of course, if you do not pay them, the seller has a right to sue you and seize whatever asset you have that would pay off those debts. But if you have spent your last nickel, the seller will have to dig into his own pocket and pay those debts he thought were taken care of. For this reason, if the seller has good advice, he will want you to sign an indemnification agreement that you are personally responsible for paying those debts.

Using the Business Debts in Your Negotiation

Keep the preceding paragraph in mind as you negotiate for the purchase of the business by assuming the seller's debts. In the usual case of a distressed business for sale, the seller's debts may be equal to or even more than the assets of the business. In that case, you should be able to buy the business just by assuming the debts. In other words, you buy it without making any down payment. If the seller objects to those terms, point out that if the deal is not accepted, she may end up with no business and obsolete equipment, but will still have the debts. Following this logic, you should question whether you should even assume all of the debts. Even though you pay nothing else, the total of the debt you assume may exceed what you have worked out to be a fair price for the business. This is where a business plan is valuable, since you can use it to demonstrate that payment of the total of the debts overvalues the business.

Buy the Business as One Package—A Corporation

This method of purchasing a business generally implies that you are buying a corporation. Although you can buy just the assets from a corporation and let the seller close up the corporation, that arrangement may not always be attractive. For instance, a corporation may own something intangible, but of significant or great value, that, for various reasons, cannot be transferred to a new owner. Specifically, this is often the case with liquor licenses for the operation of a bar and/or package store. The city or other jurisdiction may have a limit on how many licenses for the opera-tion of a bar can be in effect at the same time. If you bought just the as-sets, you would not be able to transfer the liquor license to your name, and a bar without a liquor license has little value. So, you would have to buy the corporation and do the best you can in the way of determining if there are any undisclosed corporate liabilities.

The same situation can arise when the corporation has a lease for its premises and that lease contains a clause stating that the lease is non-transferable. If the lease term includes several future years and the rent is below the current market value, it would make sense to buy the corpora-tion rather than just the assets in order to preserve the lease. This advice assumes that the lease is to the corporation as tenant, not to the owner of the business.

If you do buy the corporation, use all precautions I listed above under the topic of assuming liabilities, including the indemnification agreement. Because it is the corporation, rather than the individual owner (stock-holder) that incurred this undisclosed debt, it automatically becomes a debt that you must make sure is paid, since you now own the corporation. For that reason, the indemnification agreement takes on more importance, as does the stability and character of the seller of the corporation. If it's an individual with significant net worth who was well regarded in the com-munity, that agreement may save you a bunch of money. If the seller is someone who arrived from out of town (no one knows from where), bought the bar, operated it for a couple of years and is now selling it, you're in a dangerous situation. Spend the money for an in-depth search of the public records by your lawyer and the services of a private investi-gator to find whatever information can be had. (Perhaps you should pass on this "opportunity.")

The Business Plan

What Is a Business Plan?

If you are building your dream home, or having it built for you, the first step in that process is creating the plans for the house. It's at this stage that you are called upon to make decisions, such as, "Do I really want a larger bathroom if that will reduce the size of the master bedroom?" Obviously, it's better to make that decision at this stage rather than, weeks later, as you stand in the middle of the job site, holding up expensive tradespeople, while you decide where the wall should be put.

In a similar manner, your business is far more likely to succeed if it is built according to a plan. For instance, if you set up a kiosk in which you sell brooms in a busy shopping mall, you should do some planning. First, you set up a pricing plan. You know that the brooms will cost you $3.00 each, and you plan to sell them for $5.00 each, for a $2.00 gross profit on each broom. Then, from the national trade association of broom kiosk operators, you learn that the average kiosk sells five brooms per hour, for gross sales of $25.00 and a gross profit of $15.00 per hour. If you keep your kiosk open 10 hours per day, 7 days a week, your gross profit will be $1,050 per week. Out of that, you have expenses such as the rent charge from the mall, the part-time person to run your kiosk so you can take a little time off, plus other miscellaneous expenses, all of which add up to $750 per week, so your net profit is $300 per week. However, your mortgage payment, groceries, and automobile expenses add up to $400 per week. Obviously, the numbers in this business plan do not work, just as it does not work to try to hang a 36-inch-wide door in a 30-inch opening. In both cases, a little work at the planning stage can avoid disasters later.

Of course, this example oversimplifies the planning process. For your broom business, you can do the planning in your head. For more real-world, complex businesses, no human memory can retain all the facts and figures simultaneously. So put your business plan on paper.

Why Every Business Needs a Business Plan

Every business needs a business plan, not only for the reason above (making sure you won't go broke), but as a sales tool when you are selling others on the opportunity to earn interest or share in the profits from advancing capital to you. Those sources of capital are just as interested in your business plan as you are, and for the same reason (to determine that you will not go broke and therefore they will not go broke).

You could create a business plan for your own internal purposes on the backs of old envelopes, but when you prepare them for prospective financiers, the first impression counts. While it is you who should find reputable sources on which to base the numbers (sales volume per hour, day, or month), using professionals (accountants and other specialists) could make the difference between successfully impressing loan officers or venture capitalists and finding yourself on their reject pile.

What Is the Format of a Business Plan?

There is no prescribed format for business plans, but they generally involve the following:

- *Executive summary*: This should take up the first pages, for it summarizes all of the material included in a business plan. As you should be aware, busy bankers and venture capitalists do not have time to read every word of every business plan that floats across their desks. The executive summary helps them solve that challenge by outlining the highlights of the business plan and pinpointing and emphasizing the attractive elements (such as exceptionally high profits). A good executive summary should give the reader strong encouragement to read the whole document.

- *Description of the company*: This should include a description of the company as it now exists as well as a description of your plans for the future after you acquire it. It should list the owners of the company, the legal form of the company (corporation, LLC, etc.), the location(s) of the company's facilities, and related facts. (With a description of each of the principals, you can mention their greatest achievements, but save the detailed resume for an appendix to the business plan.)

- *Products and/or services*: This section should describe not only the present products and services of the business but projected new products and services you would offer to customers.

- *Market analysis*: This is probably the most important part of the business plan and certainly is the part that most requires substantiation. In other words, nothing else in the business plan makes any sense unless the business generates profitable sales. When you are buying a business, you can consult the records of the existing business. However, market conditions change for both better and worse, and both eventualities and their probabilities should be covered in this section.

- *Financial information*: This is probably the most arcane part of a business plan, but it is also the part that will receive the most scrutiny by a lender or investor. This is where the "what-if" questions are answered. It is where you find out that selling only five brooms per hour won't fly. It is also where an investor can determine whether you have done your homework, have determined that you must sell 15 brooms per hour, and have a well-documented marketing plan that ensures you will sell an average of 15 brooms per hour.

All of these elements are in the sample business plan that is reprinted here, courtesy of Palo Alto Software. The sample business plan is for a high-tech consulting company, so, unless that's the nature of the business you are buying, you will have to make extensive modifications to it. The sample plan was prepared with "bplan" software; I recommend using software that is designed specifically to prepare business plans. Although software is helpful in producing the whole business plan and can save you from reinventing the wheel so to speak, it is virtually a required tool for preparing the financial part of the plan. For instance, numbers in a projected profit-and-loss statement must agree with the numbers in a projected cash-flow statement. If they don't, a sophisticated investor (or the investor's accountant) will spot the error, and your dream, and the paper it's written on, will end up in the landfill. Good business plan software will make sure that your numbers are in agreement.

Using Professional Assistance in Preparing a Business Plan

You can do much of the preparation yourself; in fact, you should do much of it yourself, since it is *your* plan. Specifically, type out a draft of the entire plan. Assuming you are using business plan software, make an attempt to complete the financial area or, failing that, prepare a list of the numbers such as sales and various expenses that are based on the marketing and strategy sections of the business plan. Then have it reviewed by professionals, particularly in the areas of marketing and finance (unless you are a marketing expert or a CPA).

Do not be surprised or discouraged when you receive a telephone call from your accountant informing you that your numbers do not work. Developing a workable business plan normally involves several conversations and conferences with your accountant. (Try to use an accountant who has a little creativity and understands the process of creating a logical future financial picture.)

Please do not assume that because you are buying a business rather than starting one, you do not need projections. You, your lenders, and your investors should be more concerned with the future than with the present and past, although including the historical record of the business helps.

Help in Reading This Sample Business Plan

You can retrieve an Adobe Acrobat (.pdf) or HTML copy of the plan on the Internet at http://www.bplan.com/spv/3002/index.cfm?affiliate=pas. If that address fails to work, go to http://www.bplan.com and search for "Acme Consulting."

January, 1996

Acme Consulting—Sample Business Plan

Confidentiality Agreement

The undersigned reader acknowledges that the information provided by
.... in this business plan is confidential; therefore, reader agrees
not to disclose it without the express written permission of ....

It is acknowledged by reader that information to be furnished in this business plan is in all
respects confidential in nature, other than information which is in the public domain through
other means and that any disclosure or use of same by reader, may cause serious harm or
damage to ....

Upon request, this document is to be immediately returned to
....

....
Signature

....
Name (typed or printed)

....
Date

This is a business plan. It does not imply an offering of securities.

Acme Consulting—Sample Business Plan (Continued)

Table of Contents

Acme Consulting—Sample Business Plan (*Continued*)

Acme Consulting: © [2005] Palo Alto Software, Inc., reproduced with permission. Find more sample business plans at www.bplans.com.

1.0 Executive Summary

Acme Consulting will be a consulting company specializing in marketing of high-technology products in international markets. The company offers high-tech manufacturers a reliable, high-quality alternative to in-house resources for business development, market development, and channel development.

Acme Consulting will be created as a California C corporation based in Santa Clara County, owned by its principal investors and principal operators. The initial office will be established in A-quality office space in the Santa Clara County "Silicon Valley" area of California, the heart of the U.S. high tech industry.

Within the US and European high tech firms that Acme plans to target, we will focus on large manufacturer corporations such as HP, IBM & Microsoft. Our secondary target will be the medium-sized companies in high growth areas such as multimedia and software. One of Acme's challenges will be establishing itself as a *real* consulting company, positioned as a relatively risk-free corporate purchase.

Industry competition comes in several forms, the most significant being companies that choose to do business development and market research in-house. There are also large, well known management consulting firms such as Arthur Andersen, Boston Consulting Group, etc. These companies are generalist in nature and do not focus on a niche market. Furthermore, they are often hampered by a flawed organizational structure that does not provide the most experienced people for the client's projects. Another competitor is the various market research companies, such as Dataquest and Stanford Research Institute. Acme Consulting's advantage over such companies as these is that Acme provides high level consulting to help integrate market research data with the companies goals.

Acme Consulting will be priced at the upper edge of what the market will bear, competing with the name-brand consultants. The pricing fits with the general positioning of Acme as providing high-level expertise. Sales estimates project revenues of approximately $159,000 in the first year, and $289,000 by year 3.

The company's founders are former marketers of consulting services, personal computers, and market research, all in international markets. They are founding Acme to formalize the consulting services they offer. Acme should be managed by working partners, in a structure taken mainly from Smith Partners. In the beginning we assume 3-5 partners.

The firm estimates profits of approximately $65,000 by year 3 with a net profit margin of 6%. The company plans on taking on approximately $130,000 in current debt and raise and additional $50,000 in long-term debt to invest in long-term assets by 1998. The company does not anticipate any cash flow problems arising.

Acme Consulting—Sample Business Plan (*Continued*)

Highlights

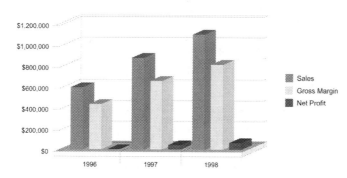

1.1 Objectives

1. Sales of $550,000 in 1996 and $1 million by 1998.
2. Gross margin higher than 70%.
3. Net income more than 5% of sales by 1998.

1.2 Mission

Acme Consulting offers high-tech manufacturers a reliable, high-quality alternative to in-house resources for business development, market development, and channel development on an international scale. A true alternative to in-house resources offers a very high level of practical experience, know-how, contacts, and confidentiality. Clients must know that working with Acme is a more professional, less risky way to develop new areas even than working completely in-house with their own people. Acme must also be able to maintain financial balance, charging a high value for its services, and delivering an even higher value to its clients. Initial focus will be development in the European and Latin American markets, or for European clients in the United States market.

Acme Consulting—Sample Business Plan (*Continued*)

Acme Consulting: © [2005] Palo Alto Software, Inc., reproduced with permission. Find more sample business plans at www.bplans.com.

1.3 Keys to Success

1. Excellence in fulfilling the promise--completely confidential, reliable, trustworthy expertise and information.
2. Developing visibility to generate new business leads.
3. Leveraging from a single pool of expertise into multiple revenue generation opportunities: retainer consulting, project consulting, market research, and market research published reports.

2.0 Company Summary

Acme Consulting is a new company providing high-level expertise in international high-tech business development, channel development, distribution strategies, and marketing of high-tech products. It will focus initially on providing two kinds of international triangles:

Providing United States clients with development for European and Latin American markets.
Providing European clients with development for the United States and Latin American markets.

As it grows it will take on people and consulting work in related markets, such as the rest of Latin America, the Far East, and similar markets. It will also look for additional leverage by taking brokerage positions and representation positions to create percentage holdings in product results.

2.1 Company Ownership

Acme Consulting will be created as a California C corporation based in Santa Clara County, owned by its principal investors and principal operators. As of this writing, it has not been chartered yet and is still considering alternatives of legal formation.

2.2 Start-up Summary

Total start-up expense (including legal costs, logo design, stationery and related expenses) comes to $18,350. Start-up assets required include $32,000 in short-term assets (office furniture, etc.) and $25,000 in initial cash to handle the first few months of consulting operations as sales and accounts receivable play through the cash flow. The details are included in Table 2-2.

Acme Consulting—Sample Business Plan (*Continued*)

Acme Consulting: © [2005] Palo Alto Software, Inc., reproduced with permission. Find more sample business plans at www.bplans.com.

Table: Start-up

Start-up

Requirements

Start-up Expenses

Legal	$1,000
Stationery etc.	$3,000
Brochures	$5,000
Consultants	$5,000
Insurance	$350
Expensed equipment	$3,000
Other	$1,000
Total Start-up Expenses	$18,350

Start-up Assets Needed

Cash Balance on Starting Date	$25,000
Other Current Assets	$7,000
Total Current Assets	$32,000
Long-term Assets	$0
Total Assets	$32,000
Total Requirements	$50,350

Funding

Investment

Investor 1	$20,000
Investor 2	$20,000
Other	$10,000
Total Investment	$50,000

Current Liabilities

Accounts Payable	$350
Current Borrowing	$0
Other Current Liabilities	$0
Current Liabilities	$350
Long-term Liabilities	$0
Total Liabilities	$350
Loss at Start-up	($18,350)
Total Capital	$31,650
Total Capital and Liabilities	$32,000

Acme Consulting—Sample Business Plan *(Continued)*

Start-up

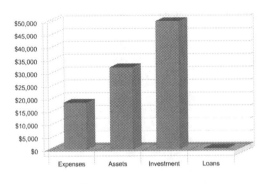

2.3 Company Locations and Facilities

The initial office will be established in A-quality office space in the Santa Clara County "Silicon Valley" area of California, the heart of the U.S. high tech industry.

3.0 Services

Acme offers the expertise a high-technology company needs to develop new product distribution and new market segments in new markets. This can be taken as high-level retainer consulting, market research reports, or project-based consulting.

3.1 Service Description

1. **Retainer consulting:** We represent a client company as an extension of its business development and market development functions. This begins with complete understanding of the client company's situation, objectives, and constraints. We then represent the client company quietly and confidentially, sifting through new market developments and new opportunities as is appropriate to the client, representing the client in initial talks with possible allies, vendors, and channels.

2. **Project consulting:** Proposed and billed on a per-project and per-milestone basis, project consulting offers a client company a way to harness our specific qualities and use our expertise to solve specific problems, develop and/or implement plans, and develop specific information.

3. **Market research:** Group studies available to selected clients at $5,000 per unit. A group study is a packaged and published complete study of a specific market, channel, or topic. Examples might be studies of developing consumer channels in Japan or Mexico, or implications of changing margins in software.

Acme Consulting—Sample Business Plan (*Continued*)

3.2 Competitive Comparison

The competition comes in several forms:

1. The most significant competition is no consulting at all, companies choosing to do business development, channel development and market research in-house. Their own managers do this on their own, as part of their regular business functions. Our key advantage in competition with in-house development is that managers are already overloaded with responsibilities, they don't have time for additional responsibilities in new market development or new channel development. Also, Acme can approach alliances, vendors, and channels on a confidential basis, gathering information and making initial contacts in ways that the corporate managers can't.

2. The high-level prestige management consulting: McKinsey, Bain, Arthur Andersen, Boston Consulting Group, etc. These are essentially generalists who take their name-brand management consulting into specialty areas. Their other very important weakness is the management structure that has the partners selling new jobs, and inexperienced associates delivering the work. We compete against them as experts in our specific fields, and with the guarantee that our clients will have the top-level people doing the actual work.

3. The third general kind of competitor is the international market research company: International Data Corporation (IDC), Dataquest, Stanford Research Institute, etc. These companies are formidable competitors for published market research and market forums, but cannot provide the kind of high-level consulting that Acme will provide.

4. The fourth kind of competition is the market-specific smaller house. For example: Nomura Research in Japan, Select S.A. de C.V. in Mexico (now affiliated with IDC).

5. Sales representation, brokering, and deal catalysts are an ad-hoc business form that will be defined in detail by the specific nature of each individual case.

3.3 Sales Literature

The business will begin with a general corporate brochure establishing the positioning. This brochure will be developed as part of the start-up expenses.

Literature and mailings for the initial market forums will be very important.

Acme Consulting—Sample Business Plan *(Continued)*

Acme Consulting: © [2005] Palo Alto Software, Inc., reproduced with permission. Find more sample business plans at www.bplans.com.

3.4 Fulfillment

1. The key fulfillment and delivery will be provided by the principals of the business. The real core value is professional expertise, provided by a combination of experience, hard work, and education (in that order).

2. We will turn to qualified professionals for freelance back-up in market research and presentation and report development, which are areas that we can afford to sub-contract without risking the core values provided to the clients.

3.5 Technology

Acme Consulting will maintain the latest Windows and Macintosh capabilities including:

1. Complete e-mail facilities on the Internet, Compuserve, America-Online, and Applelink, for working with clients directly through e-mail delivery of drafts and information.

2. Complete presentation facilities for preparation and delivery of multimedia presentations on Macintosh or Windows machines, in formats including on-disk presentation, live presentation, or video presentation.

3. Complete desktop publishing facilities for delivery of regular retainer reports, project output reports, marketing materials, and market research reports.

3.6 Future Services

In the future, Acme will broaden the coverage by expanding into coverage of additional markets (e.g., all of Latin America, Far East, Western Europe) and additional product areas (e.g., telecommunications and technology integration).

We are also studying the possibility of newsletter or electronic newsletter services, or perhaps special on-topic reports.

4.0 Market Analysis Summary

Acme will be focusing on high-technology manufacturers of computer hardware and software, services, and networking, who want to sell into markets in the United States, Europe, and Latin America. These are mostly larger companies, and occasionally medium-sized companies.

Our most important group of potential customers are executives in larger corporations. These are marketing managers, general managers, sales managers, sometimes charged with international focus and sometimes charged with market or even specific channel focus. They do not want to waste their time or risk their money looking for bargain information or questionable expertise. As they go into markets looking at new opportunities, they are very sensitive to risking their company's name and reputation.

Acme Consulting—Sample Business Plan *(Continued)*

4.1 Market Segmentation

Large manufacturer corporations: Our most important market segment is the large manufacturer of high-technology products, such as Apple, Hewlett-Packard, IBM, Microsoft, Siemens, or Olivetti. These companies will be calling on Acme for development functions that are better spun off than managed in-house, for market research, and for market forums.

Medium-sized growth companies: particularly in software, multimedia, and some related high-growth fields, Acme will offer an attractive development alternative to the company that is management constrained and unable to address opportunities in new markets and new market segments.

Market Analysis (Pie)

Table: **Market Analysis**

Market Analysis Potential Customers	Growth	1996	1997	1998	1999	2000	CAGR
U.S. High Tech	10%	5,000	5,500	6,050	6,655	7,321	10.00%
European High Tech	15%	1,000	1,150	1,323	1,521	1,749	15.00%
Latin America	35%	250	338	456	616	832	35.07%
Other	2%	10,000	10,200	10,404	10,612	10,824	2.00%
Total	6.27%	16,250	17,188	18,233	19,404	20,726	6.27%

Acme Consulting—Sample Business Plan *(Continued)*

Acme Consulting: © [2005] Palo Alto Software, Inc., reproduced with permission. Find more sample business plans at www.bplans.com.

4.2 Target Market Segment Strategy

As indicated by the previous table and Illustration, we must focus on a few thousand well-chosen potential customers in the United States, Europe, and Latin America. These few thousand high-tech manufacturing companies are the key customers for Acme.

4.3 Service Business Analysis

The consulting "industry" is pulverized and disorganized, with thousands of smaller consulting organizations and individual consultants for every one of the few dozen well-known companies.

Consulting participants range from major international name-brand consultants to tens of thousands of individuals. One of Acme's challenges will be establishing itself as a *real* consulting company, positioned as a relatively risk-free corporate purchase.

4.3.1 Business Participants

At the highest level are the few well-established major names in management consulting. Most of these are organized as partnerships established in major markets around the world, linked together by interconnecting directors and sharing the name and corporate wisdom. Some evolved from accounting companies (e.g. Arthur Andersen, Touche Ross) and some from management consulting (McKinsey, Bain). These companies charge very high rates for consulting, and maintain relatively high overhead structures and fulfillment structures based on partners selling and junior associates fulfilling.

At the intermediate level are some function-specific or market-specific consultants, such as the market research firms (IDC, Dataquest) or channel development firms (ChannelCorp, Channel Strategies, ChannelMark).

Some kinds of consulting are little more than contract expertise provided by somebody who, while temporarily out of work, offers consulting services.

4.3.2 Distributing a Service

Consulting is sold and purchased mainly on a word-of-mouth basis, with relationships and previous experience being, by far, the most important factor.

The major name-brand houses have locations in major cities and major markets, and executive-level managers or partners develop new business through industry associations, business associations, chambers of commerce and industry, etc., and in some cases social associations such as country clubs.

The medium-level houses are generally area specific or function specific, and are not easily able to leverage their business through distribution.

Acme Consulting—Sample Business Plan (*Continued*)

4.3.3 Competition and Buying Patterns

The key element in purchase decisions made at the Acme client level is trust in the professional reputation and reliability of the consulting firm.

4.3.4 Main Competitors

1. The high-level prestige management consulting:

Strengths: International locations managed by owner-partners with a high level of presentation and understanding of general business. Enviable reputations which make purchase of consulting an easy decision for a manager, despite the very high prices.

Weaknesses: General business knowledge doesn't substitute for the specific market, channel, and distribution expertise of Acme, focusing on high-technology markets and products only. Also, fees are extremely expensive, and work is generally done by very junior-level consultants, even though sold by high-level partners.

2. The international market research company:

Strengths: International offices, specific market knowledge, permanent staff developing market research information on permanent basis, good relationships with potential client companies.

Weaknesses: Market numbers are not marketing, not channel development nor market development. Although these companies compete for some of the business Acme is after, they cannot really offer the same level of business understanding at a high level.

3. Market specific or function specific experts:

Strengths: Expertise in market or functional areas. Acme should not try to compete with Nomura or Select in their markets with market research, or with ChannelCorp in channel management.

Weaknesses: The inability to spread beyond a specific focus, or to rise above a specific focus, to provide actual management expertise, experience, and wisdom beyond the specifics.

4. Companies do in-house research and development:

Strengths: No incremental cost except travel; also, the general work is done by the people who are entirely responsible. the planning is done by those who will implement it.

Weaknesses: Most managers are terribly overburdened already, unable to find incremental resources in time and people to apply to incremental opportunities. Also, there is a lot of additional risk in market and channel development done in-house from the ground up. Finally, retainer-based antenna consultants can greatly enhance a company's reach and extend its position into conversations that might otherwise never have taken place.

Acme Consulting—Sample Business Plan *(Continued)*

5.0 Strategy and Implementation Summary

Acme will focus on three geographical markets, the United States, Europe, and Latin America, and in limited product segments: personal computers, software, networks, telecommunications, personal organizers, and technology integration products.

The target customer is usually a manager in a larger corporation, and occasionally an owner or president of a medium-sized corporation in a high-growth period.

5.1 Pricing Strategy

Acme Consulting will be priced at the upper edge of what the market will bear, competing with the name-brand consultants. The pricing fits with the general positioning of Acme as providing high-level expertise.

Consulting should be based on $5,000 per day for project consulting, $2,000 per day for market research, and $10,000 per month and up for retainer consulting. Market research reports should be priced at $5,000 per report, which will, of course, require that reports be very well planned, focused on very important topics, and very well presented.

5.2 Sales Strategy

The sales forecast monthly summary is included in the appendix. The annual sales projections are included here in Table 5.2.

Sales by Year

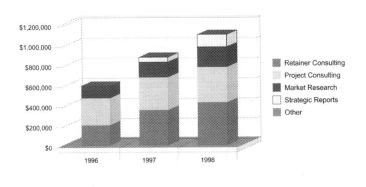

Acme Consulting—Sample Business Plan (*Continued*)

Table: Sales Forecast

Sales Forecast			
Sales	1996	1997	1998
Retainer Consulting	$200,000	$350,000	$425,000
Project Consulting	$270,000	$325,000	$350,000
Market Research	$122,000	$150,000	$200,000
Strategic Reports	$0	$50,000	$125,000
Other	$0	$0	$0
Total Sales	$592,000	$875,000	$1,100,000
Direct Cost of Sales	1996	1997	1998
Retainer Consulting	$30,000	$38,000	$48,000
Project Consulting	$45,000	$56,000	$70,000
Market Research	$84,000	$105,000	$131,000
Strategic Reports	$0	$20,000	$40,000
Other	$0	$0	$0
Subtotal Direct Cost of Sales	$159,000	$219,000	$289,000

Sales Monthly

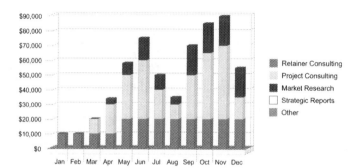

Acme Consulting—Sample Business Plan *(Continued)*

Acme Consulting: © [2005] Palo Alto Software, Inc., reproduced with permission. Find more sample business plans at www.bplans.com.

5.3 Milestones

Our detailed milestones are shown in the following table and chart. The related budgets are included with the expenses shown in the projected Profit and Loss statement, which is in the financial analysis that comes in Chapter 7 of this plan.

Milestones

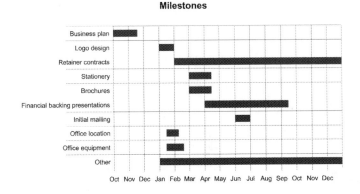

Table: Milestones

Milestones					
Milestone	Start Date	End Date	Budget	Manager	Department
Business plan	10/1/1995	11/19/1995	$5,000	HM	Devpt
Logo design	1/1/1996	2/1/1996	$2,000	TAJ	Marketing
Retainer contracts	2/1/1996	12/31/1996	$10,000	HM	Sales
Stationery	3/1/1996	4/15/1996	$500	JD	G&A
Brochures	3/1/1996	4/15/1996	$2,500	TAJ	Marketing
Financial backing presentations	4/1/1996	9/15/1996	$10,000	HM	Devpt
Initial mailing	6/1/1996	7/1/1996	$5,000	HM	Sales
Office location	1/15/1996	2/9/1996	$5,000	JD	G&A
Office equipment	1/15/1996	2/19/1996	$12,500	JD	G&A
Other	1/1/1996	12/31/1996	$10,000	ABC	Department
Totals			$62,500		

Acme Consulting—Sample Business Plan *(Continued)*

6.0 Management Summary

The initial management team depends on the founders themselves, with little back-up. As we grow, we will take on additional consulting help, plus graphic/editorial, sales, and marketing.

6.1 Organizational Structure

Acme should be managed by working partners, in a structure taken mainly from Smith Partners. In the beginning we assume 3-5 partners:

Ralph Sampson.
At least one, probably two, partners from Smith and Jones.
One strong European partner, based in Paris.
The organization has to be very flat in the beginning, with each of the founders responsible for his or her own work and management.
One other strong partner.

6.2 Management Team

The Acme business requires a very high level of international experience and expertise, which means that it will not be easily leveragable in the common consulting company mode in which partners run the business and make sales, while associates fulfill. Partners will necessarily be involved in the fulfillment of the core business proposition, providing the expertise to the clients. The initial personnel plan is still tentative. It should involve 3-5 partners, 1-3 consultants, one strong editorial/graphic person with good staff support, one strong marketing person, an office manager, and a secretary. Later, we add more partners, consultants, and sales staff. Founders' resumes are included as an attachment to this plan.

6.3 Personnel Plan

The detailed monthly personnel plan for the first year is included in the appendix. The annual personnel estimates are included here.

Table: Personnel

Personnel Plan

	1996	1997	1998
Partners	$144,000	$175,000	$200,000
Consultants	$0	$50,000	$63,000
Editorial/graphic	$18,000	$22,000	$26,000
VP Marketing	$20,000	$50,000	$55,000
Sales people	$0	$30,000	$33,000
Office Manager	$7,500	$30,000	$33,000
Secretarial	$5,250	$20,000	$22,000
Other	$0	$0	$0
Other	$0	$0	$0
Total People	7	14	20
Total Payroll	$194,750	$377,000	$432,000

Acme Consulting—Sample Business Plan (Continued)

7.0 Financial Plan

Our financial plan is based on conservative estimates and assumptions. We will need to plan on initial investment to make the financials work.

7.1 Important Assumptions

Table 7.1 summarizes key financial assumptions, including 45-day average collection days, sales entirely on invoice basis, expenses mainly on net 30 basis, 35 days on average for payment of invoices, and present-day interest rates.

Table: General Assumptions

General Assumptions

	1996	1997	1998
Plan Month	1	2	3
Current Interest Rate	8.00%	8.00%	8.00%
Long-term Interest Rate	10.00%	10.00%	10.00%
Tax Rate	25.00%	25.00%	25.00%
Sales on Credit %	100.00%	100.00%	100.00%
Other	0.00%	0.00%	0.00%
Calculated Totals			
Payroll Expense	$194,750	$377,000	$432,000
Sales on Credit	$592,000	$875,000	$1,100,000
New Accounts Payable	$498,050	$731,734	$899,115

7.2 Key Financial Indicators

The following benchmark chart indicates our key financial indicators for the first three years. We foresee major growth in sales and operating expenses, and a bump in our collection days as we spread the business during expansion.

Benchmarks

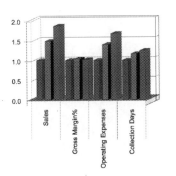

Acme Consulting—Sample Business Plan (*Continued*)

7.3 Break-even Analysis

Table 7.3 summarizes the break-even analysis, including monthly units and sales break-even points.

Break-even Analysis

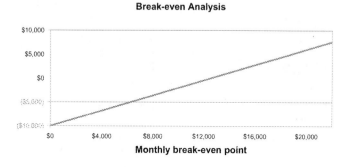

Monthly break-even point

Break-even point = where line intersects with 0

Table: Break-even Analysis

Break-even Analysis:	
Monthly Units Break-even	12,500
Monthly Revenue Break-even	$12,500
Assumptions:	
Average Per-Unit Revenue	$1.00
Average Per-Unit Variable Cost	$0.20
Estimated Monthly Fixed Cost	$10,000

Acme Consulting—Sample Business Plan *(Continued)*

7.4 Projected Profit and Loss

The detailed monthly pro-forma income statement for the first year is included in the appendix. The annual estimates are included here.

Table: Profit and Loss

Pro Forma Profit and Loss

	1996	1997	1998
Sales	$592,000	$875,000	$1,100,000
Direct Cost of Sales	$159,000	$219,000	$289,000
Other	$0	$0	$0
Total Cost of Sales	$159,000	$219,000	$289,000
Gross Margin	$433,000	$656,000	$811,000
Gross Margin %	73.14%	74.97%	73.73%
Expenses:			
Payroll	$194,750	$377,000	$432,000
Sales and Marketing and Other Expenses	$162,000	$137,000	$195,000
Depreciation	$0	$0	$0
Leased Equipment	$6,000	$7,000	$7,000
Utilities	$12,000	$12,000	$12,000
Insurance	$3,600	$2,000	$2,000
Rent	$18,000	$0	$0
Other	$0	$0	$0
Payroll Taxes	$27,265	$52,780	$60,480
Other	$0	$0	$0
Total Operating Expenses	$423,615	$587,780	$708,480
Profit Before Interest and Taxes	$9,385	$68,220	$102,520
Interest Expense	$6,800	$11,400	$15,400
Taxes Incurred	$646	$14,205	$21,780
Net Profit	$1,939	$42,615	$65,340
Net Profit/Sales	0.33%	4.87%	5.94%
Include Negative Taxes	TRUE	TRUE	TRUE

Acme Consulting—Sample Business Plan *(Continued)*

7.5 Projected Cash Flow

Cash flow projections are critical to our success. The monthly cash flow is shown in the illustration, with one bar representing the cash flow per month and the other representing the monthly balance. The annual cash flow figures are included here as Table 7.5. Detailed monthly numbers are included in the appendix.

Cash

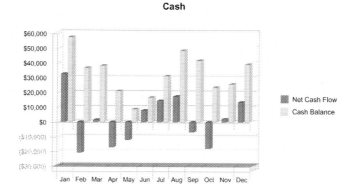

Acme Consulting—Sample Business Plan *(Continued)*

Table: Cash Flow

Pro Forma Cash Flow	1996	1997	1998
Cash Received			
Cash from Operations:			
Cash Sales	$0	$0	$0
Cash from Receivables	$495,000	$828,630	$1,063,133
Subtotal Cash from Operations	$495,000	$828,630	$1,063,133
Additional Cash Received			
Non Operating (Other) Income	$0	$0	$0
Sales Tax, VAT, HST/GST Received	$0	$0	$0
New Current Borrowing	$30,000	$100,000	$0
New Other Liabilities (interest-free)	$0	$0	$0
New Long-term Liabilities	$50,000	$0	$0
Sales of Other Current Assets	$0	$0	$0
Sales of Long-term Assets	$0	$0	$0
New Investment Received	$0	$0	$0
Subtotal Cash Received	$575,000	$928,630	$1,063,133
Expenditures	1996	1997	1998
Expenditures from Operations:			
Cash Spending	$92,012	$100,651	$135,545
Payment of Accounts Payable	$468,773	$728,952	$887,880
Subtotal Spent on Operations	$560,784	$829,603	$1,023,425
Additional Cash Spent			
Non Operating (Other) Expense	$0	$0	$0
Sales Tax, VAT, HST/GST Paid Out	$0	$0	$0
Principal Repayment of Current Borrowing	$0	$0	$0
Other Liabilities Principal Repayment	$0	$0	$0
Long-term Liabilities Principal Repayment	$0	$0	$0
Purchase Other Current Assets	$0	$0	$0
Purchase Long-term Assets	$0	$0	$0
Dividends	$0	$0	$0
Subtotal Cash Spent	$560,784	$829,603	$1,023,425
Net Cash Flow	$14,216	$99,027	$39,709
Cash Balance	$39,216	$138,243	$177,951

Acme Consulting—Sample Business Plan *(Continued)*

Acme Consulting: © [2005] Palo Alto Software, Inc., reproduced with permission. Find more sample business plans at www.bplans.com.

7.6 Projected Balance Sheet

The balance sheet shows healthy growth of net worth, and strong financial position. The monthly estimates are included in the appendix.

Table: Balance Sheet

Pro Forma Balance Sheet

Assets			
Current Assets	1996	1997	1998
Cash	$39,216	$138,243	$177,951
Accounts Receivable	$97,000	$143,370	$180,236
Other Current Assets	$7,000	$7,000	$7,000
Total Current Assets	$143,216	$288,612	$365,188
Long-term Assets			
Long-term Assets	$0	$0	$0
Accumulated Depreciation	$0	$0	$0
Total Long-term Assets	$0	$0	$0
Total Assets	$143,216	$288,612	$365,188

Liabilities and Capital			
	1996	1997	1998
Accounts Payable	$29,627	$32,409	$43,644
Current Borrowing	$30,000	$130,000	$130,000
Other Current Liabilities	$0	$0	$0
Subtotal Current Liabilities	$59,627	$162,409	$173,644
Long-term Liabilities	$50,000	$50,000	$50,000
Total Liabilities	$109,627	$212,409	$223,644
Paid-in Capital	$50,000	$50,000	$50,000
Retained Earnings	($18,350)	($16,411)	$26,204
Earnings	$1,939	$42,615	$65,340
Total Capital	$33,589	$76,204	$141,544
Total Liabilities and Capital	$143,216	$288,612	$365,188
Net Worth	$33,589	$76,204	$141,544

7.7 Business Ratios

The following table shows the projected business ratios. We expect to maintain healthy ratios for profitability, risk, and return. The industry comparisons are for SIC 8742, management consulting services.

Acme Consulting—Sample Business Plan *(Continued)*

Acme Consulting: © [2005] Palo Alto Software, Inc., reproduced with permission. Find more sample business plans at www.bplans.com.

Table: Ratios

Ratio Analysis

	1996	1997	1998	Industry Profile
Sales Growth	0.00%	47.80%	25.71%	6.98%
Percent of Total Assets				
Accounts Receivable	67.73%	49.68%	49.35%	26.80%
Inventory	0.00%	0.00%	0.00%	5.01%
Other Current Assets	4.89%	2.43%	1.92%	43.95%
Total Current Assets	100.00%	100.00%	100.00%	75.76%
Long-term Assets	0.00%	0.00%	0.00%	24.24%
Total Assets	100.00%	100.00%	100.00%	100.00%
Current Liabilities	41.63%	56.27%	47.55%	31.78%
Long-term Liabilities	34.91%	17.32%	13.69%	17.26%
Total Liabilities	76.55%	73.60%	61.24%	49.04%
Net Worth	23.45%	26.40%	38.76%	50.96%
Percent of Sales				
Sales	100.00%	100.00%	100.00%	100.00%
Gross Margin	73.14%	74.97%	73.73%	100.00%
Selling, General & Administrative Expenses	72.81%	70.10%	67.79%	85.31%
Advertising Expenses	6.08%	4.57%	4.00%	1.02%
Profit Before Interest and Taxes	1.59%	7.80%	9.32%	1.90%
Main Ratios				
Current	2.40	1.78	2.10	1.88
Quick	2.40	1.78	2.10	1.48
Total Debt to Total Assets	76.55%	73.60%	61.24%	3.41%
Pre-tax Return on Net Worth	7.70%	74.56%	61.55%	55.78%
Pre-tax Return on Assets	1.80%	19.69%	23.86%	7.72%

Business Vitality Profile	1996	1997	1998	Industry
Sales per Employee	$84,571	$62,500	$55,000	$0
Survival Rate				0.00%

Additional Ratios	1996	1997	1998	
Net Profit Margin	0.33%	4.87%	5.94%	n.a
Return on Equity	5.77%	55.92%	46.16%	n.a
Activity Ratios				
Accounts Receivable Turnover	6.10	6.10	6.10	n.a
Collection Days	43	50	54	n.a
Inventory Turnover	0.00	0.00	0.00	n.a
Accounts Payable Turnover	16.81	22.58	20.60	n.a
Payment Days	17	15	15	n.a
Total Asset Turnover	4.13	3.03	3.01	n.a
Debt Ratios				
Debt to Net Worth	3.26	2.79	1.58	n.a
Current Liab. to Liab.	0.54	0.76	0.78	n.a
Liquidity Ratios				
Net Working Capital	$83,589	$126,204	$191,544	n.a
Interest Coverage	1.38	5.98	6.66	n.a
Additional Ratios				
Assets to Sales	0.24	0.33	0.33	n.a
Current Debt/Total Assets	42%	56%	48%	n.a
Acid Test	0.78	0.89	1.07	n.a
Sales/Net Worth	17.62	11.48	7.77	n.a
Dividend Payout	0.00	0.00	0.00	n.a

Acme Consulting—Sample Business Plan *(Continued)*

Appendix Table: Sales Forecast

Sales Forecast

	Jan	Feb	Mar	Apr	May	Jun	Jul	Aug	Sep	Oct	Nov	Dec
Sales												
Retainer Consulting	$10,000	$10,000	$10,000	$10,000	$20,000	$20,000	$20,000	$20,000	$20,000	$20,000	$20,000	$20,000
Project Consulting	$0	$0	$10,000	$20,000	$30,000	$40,000	$20,000	$10,000	$30,000	$45,000	$50,000	$15,000
Market Research	$0	$0	$0	$4,000	$8,000	$15,000	$10,000	$5,000	$20,000	$20,000	$20,000	$20,000
Strategic Reports	$0	$0	$0	$0	$0	$0	$0	$0	$0	$0	$0	$0
Other	$0	$0	$0	$0	$0	$0	$0	$0	$0	$0	$0	$0
Total Sales	$10,000	$10,000	$20,000	$34,000	$58,000	$75,000	$50,000	$35,000	$70,000	$85,000	$90,000	$55,000

	Jan	Feb	Mar	Apr	May	Jun	Jul	Aug	Sep	Oct	Nov	Dec
Direct Cost of Sales												
Retainer Consulting	$2,500	$2,500	$2,500	$2,500	$2,500	$2,500	$2,500	$2,500	$2,500	$2,500	$2,500	$2,500
Project Consulting	$0	$0	$1,500	$3,500	$5,000	$6,500	$3,500	$1,500	$5,000	$7,500	$8,500	$2,500
Market Research	$0	$0	$0	$2,000	$6,000	$10,000	$6,000	$4,000	$14,000	$14,000	$14,000	$14,000
Strategic Reports	$0	$0	$0	$0	$0	$0	$0	$0	$0	$0	$0	$0
Other	$0	$0	$0	$0	$0	$0	$0	$0	$0	$0	$0	$0
Subtotal Direct Cost of Sales	$2,500	$2,500	$4,000	$8,000	$13,500	$19,000	$12,000	$8,000	$21,500	$24,000	$25,000	$19,000

Acme Consulting—Sample Business Plan (Continued)

Acme Consulting: © [2005] Palo Alto Software, Inc., reproduced with permission. Find more sample business plans at www.bplans.com.

Appendix

Appendix Table: Personnel

Personnel Plan		Jan	Feb	Mar	Apr	May	Jun	Jul	Aug	Sep	Oct	Nov	Dec
Partners	$1	$12,000	$12,000	$12,000	$12,000	$12,000	$12,000	$12,000	$12,000	$12,000	$12,000	$12,000	$12,000
Consultants	$1	$0	$0	$0	$0	$0	$0	$0	$0	$0	$0	$6,000	$6,000
Editorial/graphic	$1	$0	$0	$0	$0	$0	$0	$0	$0	$5,000	$6,000	$6,000	$6,000
VP Marketing	$1	$0	$0	$0	$0	$0	$0	$0	$0	$5,000	$5,000	$5,000	$5,000
Sales people	$1	$0	$0	$0	$0	$0	$0	$0	$0	$0	$0	$0	$0
Office Manager	$1	$0	$0	$0	$0	$0	$0	$0	$0	$0	$2,500	$2,500	$2,500
Secretarial	$1	$0	$0	$0	$0	$0	$0	$0	$0	$0	$1,750	$1,750	$1,750
Other		$0	$0	$0	$0	$0	$0	$0	$0	$0	$0	$0	$0
Other		$0	$0	$0	$0	$0	$0	$0	$0	$0	$0	$0	$0
Total People		3	3	3	3	3	3	3	3	5	7	7	7
Total Payroll		$12,000	$12,000	$12,000	$12,000	$12,000	$12,000	$12,000	$12,000	$17,000	$27,250	$27,250	$27,250

Acme Consulting—Sample Business Plan (*Continued*)

Acme Consulting: © [2005] Palo Alto Software, Inc., reproduced with permission. Find more sample business plans at www.bplans.com.

Appendix Table: General Assumptions

General Assumptions

	Jan 1	Feb 2	Mar 3	Apr 4	May 5	Jun 6	Jul 7	Aug 8	Sep 9	Oct 10	Nov 11	Dec 12
Plan Month	1	2	3	4	5	6	7	8	9	10	11	12
Current Interest Rate	8.00%	8.00%	8.00%	8.00%	8.00%	8.00%	8.00%	8.00%	8.00%	8.00%	8.00%	8.00%
Long-term Interest Rate	10.00%	10.00%	10.00%	10.00%	10.00%	10.00%	10.00%	10.00%	10.00%	10.00%	10.00%	10.00%
Tax Rate	25.00%	25.00%	25.00%	25.00%	25.00%	25.00%	25.00%	25.00%	25.00%	25.00%	25.00%	25.00%
Sales on Credit %	100.00%	100.00%	100.00%	100.00%	100.00%	100.00%	100.00%	100.00%	100.00%	100.00%	100.00%	100.00%
Other	0.00%	0.00%	0.00%	0.00%	0.00%	0.00%	0.00%	0.00%	0.00%	0.00%	0.00%	0.00%
Calculated Totals												
Payroll Expense	$12,000	$12,000	$12,000	$12,000	$12,000	$12,000	$12,000	$12,000	$17,000	$27,250	$27,250	$27,250
Sales on Credit	$10,000	$10,000	$20,000	$34,000	$58,000	$75,000	$50,000	$35,000	$70,000	$85,000	$90,000	$55,000
New Accounts Payable	$24,081	$24,081	$26,874	$31,749	$39,343	$45,662	$37,037	$31,974	$50,762	$64,475	$65,975	$56,037

Acme Consulting—Sample Business Plan (*Continued*)

Appendix

Appendix Table: Profit and Loss

Pro Forma Profit and Loss

	Jan	Feb	Mar	Apr	May	Jun	Jul	Aug	Sep	Oct	Nov	Dec
Sales	$10,000	$10,000	$20,000	$34,000	$58,000	$75,000	$50,000	$35,000	$70,000	$85,000	$90,000	$55,000
Direct Cost of Sales	$2,500	$2,500	$4,000	$8,000	$13,500	$19,000	$12,000	$8,000	$21,500	$24,000	$25,000	$19,000
Other	$0	$0	$0	$0	$0	$0	$0	$0	$0	$0	$0	$0
Total Cost of Sales	$2,500	$2,500	$4,000	$8,000	$13,500	$19,000	$12,000	$8,000	$21,500	$24,000	$25,000	$19,000
Gross Margin	$7,500	$7,500	$16,000	$26,000	$44,500	$56,000	$38,000	$27,000	$48,500	$61,000	$65,000	$36,000
Gross Margin %	75.00%	75.00%	80.00%	76.47%	76.72%	74.67%	76.00%	77.14%	69.29%	71.76%	72.22%	65.45%
Expenses:												
Payroll	$12,000	$12,000	$12,000	$12,000	$12,000	$12,000	$12,000	$12,000	$17,000	$27,250	$27,250	$27,250
Sales and Marketing and Other Expenses	$13,500	$13,500	$13,500	$13,500	$13,500	$13,500	$13,500	$13,500	$13,500	$13,500	$13,500	$13,500
Depreciation	$0	$0	$0	$0	$0	$0	$0	$0	$0	$0	$0	$0
Leased Equipment	$500	$500	$500	$500	$500	$500	$500	$500	$500	$500	$500	$500
Utilities	$1,000	$1,000	$1,000	$1,000	$1,000	$1,000	$1,000	$1,000	$1,000	$1,000	$1,000	$1,000
Insurance	$300	$300	$300	$300	$300	$300	$300	$300	$300	$300	$300	$300
Rent	$1,500	$1,500	$1,500	$1,500	$1,500	$1,500	$1,500	$1,500	$1,500	$1,500	$1,500	$1,500
Payroll Taxes 14%	$1,680	$1,680	$1,680	$1,680	$1,680	$1,680	$1,680	$1,680	$2,380	$3,815	$3,815	$3,815
Other	$0	$0	$0	$0	$0	$0	$0	$0	$0	$0	$0	$0
Total Operating Expenses	$30,480	$30,480	$30,480	$30,480	$30,480	$30,480	$30,480	$30,480	$36,180	$47,865	$47,865	$47,865
Profit Before Interest and Taxes	($22,980)	($22,980)	($14,480)	($4,480)	$14,020	$25,520	$7,520	($3,480)	$12,320	$13,135	$17,135	($11,865)
Interest Expense	$417	$417	$417	$550	$550	$617	$617	$617	$617	$617	$617	$617
Taxes Incurred	($5,849)	($5,849)	($3,758)	($1,258)	$3,368	$6,226	$1,726	($1,024)	$2,926	$3,130	$4,130	($3,120)
Net Profit	($17,548)	($17,548)	($11,273)	($3,773)	$10,103	$18,678	$5,178	($3,073)	$8,778	$9,389	$12,389	($9,361)
Net Profit/Sales	-175.48%	-175.48%	-56.36%	-11.10%	17.42%	24.90%	10.36%	-8.78%	12.54%	11.05%	13.77%	-17.02%
Include Negative Taxes												

Acme Consulting—Sample Business Plan (*Continued*)

Acme Consulting: © [2005] Palo Alto Software, Inc., reproduced with permission. Find more sample business plans at www.bplans.com.

Appendix Table: Cash Flow

Pro Forma Cash Flow		Jan	Feb	Mar	Apr	May	Jun	Jul	Aug	Sep	Oct	Nov	Dec
Cash Received													
Cash from Operations:													
Cash Sales		$0	$0	$0	$0	$0	$0	$0	$0	$0	$0	$0	$0
Cash from Receivables		$0	$5,333	$10,000	$15,333	$27,467	$46,800	$67,067	$61,667	$42,000	$53,667	$78,000	$87,667
Subtotal Cash from Operations		$0	$5,333	$10,000	$15,333	$27,467	$46,800	$67,067	$61,667	$42,000	$53,667	$78,000	$87,667
Additional Cash Received													
Non Operating (Other) Income	0.00%	$0	$0	$0	$0	$0	$0	$0	$0	$0	$0	$0	$0
Sales Tax, VAT, HST/GST Received		$0	$0	$0	$0	$0	$0	$0	$0	$0	$0	$0	$0
New Current Borrowing		$0	$0	$20,000	$0	$0	$10,000	$0	$0	$0	$0	$0	$0
New Other Liabilities (interest-free)		$0	$0	$0	$0	$0	$0	$0	$0	$0	$0	$0	$0
New Long-term Liabilities		$50,000	$0	$0	$0	$0	$0	$0	$0	$0	$0	$0	$0
Sales of Other Current Assets		$0	$0	$0	$0	$0	$0	$0	$0	$0	$0	$0	$0
Sales of Long-term Assets		$0	$0	$0	$0	$0	$0	$0	$0	$0	$0	$0	$0
New Investment Received		$0	$0	$0	$0	$0	$0	$0	$0	$0	$0	$0	$0
Subtotal Cash Received		$60,000	$5,333	$30,000	$15,333	$27,467	$56,800	$67,067	$61,667	$42,000	$53,667	$78,000	$87,667
Expenditures		Jan	Feb	Mar	Apr	May	Jun	Jul	Aug	Sep	Oct	Nov	Dec
Expenditures from Operations:													
Cash Spending		$3,467	$3,467	$4,398	$6,023	$8,554	$10,661	$7,786	$6,098	$10,461	$11,137	$11,637	$8,324
Payment of Accounts Payable		$13,980	$22,737	$24,088	$26,502	$31,099	$38,331	$44,819	$38,187	$38,349	$60,702	$64,204	$65,775
Subtotal Spent on Operations		$17,447	$26,204	$28,486	$32,525	$39,654	$48,991	$52,605	$44,285	$48,810	$71,838	$75,841	$74,099
Additional Cash Spent													
Non Operating (Other) Expense		$0	$0	$0	$0	$0	$0	$0	$0	$0	$0	$0	$0
Sales Tax, VAT, HST/GST Paid Out		$0	$0	$0	$0	$0	$0	$0	$0	$0	$0	$0	$0
Principal Repayment of Current Borrowing		$0	$0	$0	$0	$0	$0	$0	$0	$0	$0	$0	$0
Other Liabilities Principal Repayment		$0	$0	$0	$0	$0	$0	$0	$0	$0	$0	$0	$0
Long-term Liabilities Principal Repayment		$0	$0	$0	$0	$0	$0	$0	$0	$0	$0	$0	$0
Purchase Other Current Assets		$0	$0	$0	$0	$0	$0	$0	$0	$0	$0	$0	$0
Purchase Long-term Assets		$0	$0	$0	$0	$0	$0	$0	$0	$0	$0	$0	$0
Dividends		$0	$0	$0	$0	$0	$0	$0	$0	$0	$0	$0	$0
Subtotal Cash Spent		$17,447	$26,204	$28,486	$32,525	$39,654	$48,991	$52,605	$44,285	$48,810	$71,838	$75,841	$74,099
Net Cash Flow		$32,553	($20,870)	$1,514	($17,192)	($12,187)	$7,809	$14,462	$17,382	($6,810)	($18,172)	$2,159	$13,568
Cash Balance		$57,553	$36,683	$38,197	$21,005	$8,818	$16,627	$31,089	$48,470	$41,660	$23,489	$25,648	$39,216

Acme Consulting—Sample Business Plan (Continued)

Acme Consulting: © [2005] Palo Alto Software, Inc., reproduced with permission. Find more sample business plans at www.bplans.com.

Appendix

Appendix Table: Balance Sheet

Pro Forma Balance Sheet

	Starting Balances	Jan	Feb	Mar	Apr	May	Jun	Jul	Aug	Sep	Oct	Nov	Dec
Assets													
Current Assets													
Cash	$25,600	$57,553	$36,683	$38,197	$21,005	$8,818	$16,627	$31,089	$48,470	$41,660	$23,489	$25,648	$39,216
Accounts Receivable	$0	$10,000	$14,667	$24,667	$43,333	$73,867	$102,067	$85,000	$58,333	$86,333	$117,667	$129,667	$97,000
Other Current Assets	$7,000	$7,000	$7,000	$7,000	$7,000	$7,000	$7,000	$7,000	$7,000	$7,000	$7,000	$7,000	$7,000
Total Current Assets	$32,000	$74,553	$58,350	$69,864	$71,339	$89,685	$125,694	$123,089	$113,804	$134,994	$148,155	$162,314	$143,216
Long-term Assets													
Long-term Assets	$0	$0	$0	$0	$0	$0	$0	$0	$0	$0	$0	$0	$0
Accumulated Depreciation	$0	$0	$0	$0	$0	$0	$0	$0	$0	$0	$0	$0	$0
Total Long-term Assets	$0	$0	$0	$0	$0	$0	$0	$0	$0	$0	$0	$0	$0
Total Assets	$32,000	$74,553	$58,350	$69,864	$71,339	$89,685	$125,694	$123,089	$113,804	$134,994	$148,155	$162,314	$143,216

	Starting Balances	Jan	Feb	Mar	Apr	May	Jun	Jul	Aug	Sep	Oct	Nov	Dec
Liabilities and Capital													
Accounts Payable	$350	$10,451	$11,795	$14,581	$19,829	$28,072	$35,404	$27,621	$21,409	$33,821	$37,594	$39,364	$29,627
Current Borrowing	$0	$0	$0	$20,000	$20,000	$20,000	$30,000	$30,000	$30,000	$30,000	$30,000	$30,000	$30,000
Other Current Liabilities	$0	$0	$0	$0	$0	$0	$0	$0	$0	$0	$0	$0	$0
Subtotal Current Liabilities	$350	$10,451	$11,795	$34,581	$39,829	$48,072	$65,404	$57,621	$51,409	$63,821	$67,594	$69,364	$59,627
Long-term Liabilities	$0	$50,000	$50,000	$50,000	$50,000	$50,000	$50,000	$50,000	$50,000	$50,000	$50,000	$50,000	$50,000
Total Liabilities	$350	$60,451	$61,795	$84,581	$89,829	$98,072	$115,404	$107,621	$101,409	$113,821	$117,594	$119,364	$109,627
Paid-in Capital	$50,000	$50,000	$50,000	$50,000	$50,000	$50,000	$50,000	$50,000	$50,000	$50,000	$50,000	$50,000	$50,000
Retained Earnings	($18,350)	($18,350)	($18,350)	($18,350)	($18,350)	($18,350)	($18,350)	($18,350)	($18,350)	($18,350)	($18,350)	($18,350)	($18,350)
Earnings	$0	($17,548)	($35,095)	($46,368)	($50,140)	($40,036)	($21,360)	($16,183)	($19,255)	($10,478)	($1,089)	$11,300	$1,939
Total Capital	$31,650	$14,103	($3,445)	($14,718)	($18,490)	($8,388)	$10,290	$15,468	$12,395	$21,173	$30,561	$42,950	$33,589
Total Liabilities and Capital	$32,000	$74,553	$58,350	$69,864	$71,339	$89,685	$125,694	$123,089	$113,804	$134,994	$148,155	$162,314	$143,216
Net Worth	$31,650	$14,103	($3,445)	($14,718)	($18,490)	($8,388)	$10,290	$15,468	$12,395	$21,173	$30,561	$42,950	$33,589

Acme Consulting—Sample Business Plan (Continued)

Acme Consulting: © [2005] Palo Alto Software, Inc., reproduced with permission. Find more sample business plans at www.bplans.com.

Finding Investors and Navigating the Regulations

Chapter 4 covers the possibility that you can finance the purchase of a business by selling a share of your business to other people or institutions of various means and sophistication. Relative to that, this appendix includes:

- A question-and answer-brochure published by the SEC, which covers the simplified registration procedures for small businesses that raise cash by selling part of the ownership of the business.

- Frequently asked questions (FAQs) about Active Capital.

- Addresses and phone numbers of state securities regulations administrators.

Securities and Exchange Commission Brochure

U.S. Securities and Exchange Commission

Q&A: Small Business and the SEC

A guide to help you understand how to raise capital and comply with the federal securities laws

May 1999

Table of Contents

SEC Brochure

I. What Are the Federal Securities Laws?

In the chaotic securities markets of the 1920s, companies often sold stocks and bonds on the basis of glittering promises of fantastic profits - without disclosing any meaningful information to investors. These conditions contributed to the disastrous Stock Market Crash of 1929. In response, the U.S. Congress enacted the federal securities laws and created the Securities and Exchange Commission (SEC) to administer them.

There are two primary sets of federal laws that come into play when a company wants to offer and sell its securities to the public. They are:

- the Securities Act of 1933 (Securities Act), and
- the Securities Exchange Act of 1934 (Exchange Act).

Securities Act

The Securities Act generally requires companies to give investors "full disclosure" of all "material facts," the facts investors would find important in making an investment decision. This Act also requires companies to file a registration statement with the SEC that includes information for investors. The SEC does not evaluate the merits of offerings, or determine if the securities offered are "good" investments. The SEC staff reviews registration statements and declares them "effective" if companies satisfy our disclosure rules. We describe this process in more detail beginning on page 7.

Exchange Act

The Exchange Act requires publicly held companies to disclose information continually about their business operations, financial conditions, and managements. These companies, and in many cases their officers, directors and significant shareholders, must file periodic reports or other disclosure documents with the SEC. In some cases, the company must deliver the information directly to investors. We discuss these obligations more fully beginning on page 11.

Exemptions

Your company may be exempt from these registration and reporting requirements. We discuss exemptions beginning on page 16.

II. How Can I Get Answers to My Questions?

The SEC tries to meet the needs of small business through its rules and regulations. It also offers informal guidance by answering your questions over the phone, through the mail or by e-mail. The SEC offers you a number of ways to express your views and get help from the staff. Of course, you should always retain competent counsel before engaging in any securities offering.

Special Ombudsman to Serve You

http://www.sec.gov/info/smallbus/qasbsec.htm

SEC Brochure (*Continued*)

In 1996, we appointed a Special Ombudsman for Small Business to serve you and to represent the concerns of smaller companies within the SEC. You can tell the Ombudsman your concerns about any SEC proposal or rule. The Ombudsman also can answer your general questions or help you find the answers to your specific questions. The Ombudsman's telephone number is (202) 942-2950.

The Office of Small Business

The Division of Corporation Finance's Office of Small Business directs the SEC's small business rulemaking initiatives and comments on SEC rule proposals affecting small companies. Its staff works with Congressional committees, government agencies, and other groups concerned with small business. The Office also specializes in the review of filings from small companies. Its telephone number is (202) 942-2950.

Town Hall Meetings

The Office of Small Business also sponsors small business town hall meetings across the country. These meetings help the SEC convey basic information to small businesses and learn more about the problems small businesses face in raising capital. These meetings help the SEC design programs that meet small businesses' needs while protecting investors.

Government-Business Forum on Small Business Capital Formation

In addition to the town hall meetings, the SEC sponsors the Government-Business Forum on Small Business Capital Formation. This annual meeting provides the only national forum for small businesses to let government officials from different parts of the federal government know how the laws, rules and regulations impact the ability of small companies to raise capital. You can get more information about this forum from the Office of Small Business.

Internet Web Site

We also maintain a home page on the World Wide Web at http://www.sec.gov. Our site includes recent SEC releases and other updating information of interest to small companies. Through our Web site, small companies and investors can also find documents publicly filed on the SEC's Electronic Data Gathering, Analysis, and Retrieval, or EDGAR, system. Most registration statements and other documents must now be filed electronically via that system.

III. Should My Company "Go Public"?

When your company needs additional capital, "going public" may be the right choice, but you should weigh your options carefully. If your company is in the very early stages of development, it may be better to seek loans from financial institutions or the Small Business Administration. Other alternatives include raising money by selling securities in transactions that are exempt from the registration process. We discuss these alternatives later.

http://www.sec.gov/info/smallbus/qasbsec.htm

SEC Brochure *(Continued)*

There are benefits and new obligations that come from raising capital through a public offering registered with the SEC. While the benefits are attractive, be sure you are ready to assume these new obligations:

Benefits

- Your access to capital will increase, since you can contact more potential investors.
- Your company may become more widely known.
- You may obtain financing more easily in the future if investor interest in your company grows enough to sustain a secondary trading market in your securities.
- Controlling shareholders, such as the company's officers or directors, may have a ready market for their shares, which means that they can more easily sell their interests at retirement, for diversification, or for some other reason.
- Your company may be able to attract and retain more highly qualified personnel if it can offer stock options, bonuses, or other incentives with a known market value.
- The image of your company may be improved.

New Obligations

- You must continue to keep shareholders informed about the company's business operations, financial condition, and management, incurring additional costs and new legal obligations.
- You may be liable if you do not fulfill these new legal obligations.
- You may lose some flexibility in managing your company's affairs, particularly when shareholders must approve your actions.
- Your public offering will take time and money to accomplish.

IV. How Does My Small Business Register a Public Offering?

If you decide on a registered public offering, the Securities Act requires your company to file a registration statement with the SEC before the company can offer its securities for sale. You cannot actually sell the securities covered by the registration statement until the SEC staff declares it "effective," even though registration statements become public immediately upon filing.

Registration statements have two principal parts:

- Part I is the prospectus, the legal offering or "selling" document. Your company - the "issuer" of the securities - must describe in the prospectus the important facts about its business operations, financial condition, and management. Everyone who buys the new issue, as well as anyone who is made an offer to purchase the securities, must have access to the prospectus.
- Part II contains additional information that the company does not have to deliver to investors. Anyone can see this information by requesting it from one of the SEC's public reference rooms or by looking it up on the SEC Web site.

The Basic Registration Form - Form S-1

http://www.sec.gov/info/smallbus/qasbsec.htm

SEC Brochure (Continued)

All companies can use Form S-1 to register their securities offerings. You should not prepare a registration statement as a fill-in-the-blank form, like a tax return. It should be similar to a brochure, providing readable information. If you file this form, your company must describe each of the following in the prospectus:

- its business;
- its properties;
- its competition;
- the identity of its officers and directors and their compensation;
- material transactions between the company and its officers and directors;
- material legal proceedings involving the company or its officers and directors;
- the plan for distributing the securities; and the intended use of the proceeds of the offering.

Information about how to describe these items is set out in SEC rules. Registration statements also must include financial statements audited by an independent certified public accountant.

In addition to the information expressly required by the form, your company must also provide any other information that is necessary to make your disclosure complete and not misleading. You also must clearly describe any risks prominently in the prospectus, usually at the beginning. Examples of these risk factors are:

- lack of business operating history;
- adverse economic conditions in a particular industry;
- lack of a market for the securities offered; and
- dependence upon key personnel.

Alternative Registration Forms for Small Business Issuers

If your company qualifies as a "small business issuer," it can choose to file its registration statement using one of the simplified small business forms. A small business issuer is a United States or Canadian issuer:

- that had less than $25 million in revenues in its last fiscal year, and
- whose outstanding publicly-held stock is worth no more than $25 million.

Form SB-1 - To Raise $10 Million or Less

Small business issuers offering up to $10 million worth of securities in any 12-month period may use Form SB1. This form allows you to provide information in a question and answer format, similar to that used in Regulation A offerings, a type of exempt offering discussed on page 19. Unlike Regulation A filings, Form SB-1 requires audited financial statements.

Form SB-2 - To Raise Capital in Any Amount

If your company is a "small business issuer," it may register an unlimited dollar amount of securities using Form SB-2, and may use this form again and again so long as it satisfies the "small business issuer" definition.

http://www.sec.gov/info/smallbus/qasbsec.htm

SEC Brochure (Continued)

One advantage of Form SB-2 is that all its disclosure requirements are in Regulation S-B, a set of rules written in simple, non-legalistic terminology. Form SB-2 also permits the company to:

- Provide audited financial statements, prepared according to generally accepted accounting principles, for two fiscal years. In contrast, Form S-1 requires the issuer to provide audited financial statements, prepared according to more detailed SEC regulations, for three fiscal years; and
- Include less extensive narrative disclosure than Form S-1 requires, particularly in the description of your business, and executive compensation.

Staff Review of Registration Statements

SEC staff examines registration statements for compliance with disclosure requirements. If a filing appears incomplete or inaccurate, the staff usually informs the company by letter. The company may file correcting or clarifying amendments. Once the company has satisfied the disclosure requirements, the staff declares the registration statement effective. The company may then begin to sell its securities. The SEC can refuse or suspend the effectiveness of any registration statement if it concludes that the document is misleading, inaccurate, or incomplete.

V. If My Company Becomes Public, What Disclosures Must I Regularly Make?

Your company can become "public" in one of two ways - by issuing securities in an offering registered under the Securities Act or by registering the company's outstanding securities under Exchange Act requirements. Both types of registration trigger ongoing reporting obligations for your company. In some cases, the Exchange Act also subjects your company's officers, directors and significant shareholders to reporting requirements. Let's discuss these requirements individually.

Reporting obligations because of Securities Act registration

Once the staff declares your company's Securities Act registration statement effective, the Exchange Act requires you to file reports with the SEC. The obligation to file reports continues at least through the end of the fiscal year in which your registration statement becomes effective. After that, you are required to continue reporting unless you satisfy the following "thresholds," in which case your filing obligations are suspended:

- your company has fewer than 300 shareholders of the class of securities offered; or
- your company has fewer than 500 shareholders of the class of securities offered and less than $10 million in total assets for each of its last three fiscal years.

If your company is subject to the reporting requirements, it must file information with the SEC about:

- its operations;

http://www.sec.gov/info/smallbus/qasbsec.htm

SEC Brochure (*Continued*)

- its officers, directors, and certain shareholders, including salary, various fringe benefits, and transactions between the company and management;
- the financial condition of the business, including financial statements audited by an independent certified public accountant; and
- its competitive position and material terms of contracts or lease agreements.

All of this information becomes publicly available when you file your reports with the SEC. As is true with Securities Act filings, small business issuers may choose to use small business alternative forms and Regulation S-B for registration and reporting under the Exchange Act.

Obligations because of Exchange Act registration

Even if your company has not registered a securities offering, it must file an Exchange Act registration statement if:

- it has more than $10 million total assets and a class of equity securities, like common stock, with 500 or more shareholders; or
- it lists its securities on an exchange or on Nasdaq.

If a class of your company's securities is registered under the Exchange Act, the company, as well as its shareholders and management, are subject to various reporting requirements, explained below.

Ongoing Exchange Act periodic reporting

If your company registers a class of securities under the Exchange Act, it must file the same annual, periodic, and current reports that are required as a result of Securities Act registration, as explained above. This obligation continues for as long as the company exceeds the reporting thresholds previously outlined on page 11. If your company's securities are traded on an exchange or on Nasdaq, the company must continue filing these reports as long as the securities trade on those markets, even if your company falls below the thresholds.

Proxy rules

A company with Exchange Act registered securities must comply with the SEC's proxy rules whenever it seeks a shareholder vote on corporate matters. These rules require the company to provide a proxy statement to its shareholders, together with a proxy card when soliciting proxies. Proxy statements discuss management and executive compensation, along with descriptions of the matters up for a vote. If the company is not soliciting proxies but will take a vote on a matter, the company must provide to its shareholders an information statement that is similar to a proxy statement. The proxy rules also require your company to send an annual report to shareholders if there will be an election of directors. These reports contain much of the same information found in the Exchange Act annual reports that a company must file with the SEC, including audited financial statements. The proxy rules also govern when your company must provide shareholder lists to investors and when it must include a shareholder proposal in the proxy statement.

Beneficial ownership reports

http://www.sec.gov/info/smallbus/qasbsec.htm

SEC Brochure (Continued)

If your company has registered a class of its equity securities under the Exchange Act, persons who acquire more than five percent of the outstanding shares of that class must file beneficial owner reports until their holdings drop below five percent. These filings contain background information about the beneficial owners as well as their investment intentions, providing investors and the company with information about accumulations of securities that may potentially change or influence company management and policies.

Tender offers

A public company with Exchange Act registered securities that faces a takeover attempt, or third party tender offer, should be aware that the SEC's tender offer rules will apply to the transaction. The same is true if the company makes a tender offer for its own Exchange Act registered securities. The filings required by these rules provide information to the public about the person making the tender offer. The company that is the subject of the takeover must file with the SEC its responses to the tender offer. The rules also set time limits for the tender offer and provide other protections to shareholders.

Transaction reporting by officers, directors and ten percent shareholders

Section 16 of the Exchange Act applies to your company's directors and officers, as well as shareholders who own more than 10% of a class of your company's equity securities registered under the Exchange Act. It requires these persons to report their transactions involving the company's equity securities to the SEC. Section 16 also establishes mechanisms for a company to recover "short swing" profits, those profits an insider realizes from a purchase and sale of a company security within a six-month period. In addition, Section 16 prohibits short selling by these persons of any class of the company's securities, whether or not that class is registered under the Exchange Act.

VI. Are There Legal Ways To Offer and Sell Securities Without Registering With the SEC?

Yes! Your company's securities offering may qualify for one of several exemptions from the registration requirements. We explain the most common ones below. You must remember, however, that all securities transactions, even exempt transactions, are subject to the antifraud provisions of the federal securities laws. This means that you and your company will be responsible for false or misleading statements, whether oral or written. The government enforces the federal securities laws through criminal, civil and administrative proceedings. Some enforcement proceedings are brought through private law suits. Also, if all conditions of the exemptions are not met, purchasers may be able to obtain refunds of their purchase price. In addition, offerings that are exempt from provisions of the federal securities laws may still be subject to the notice and filing obligations of various state laws. Make sure you check with the appropriate state securities administrator before proceeding with your offering.

A. Intrastate Offering Exemption

http://www.sec.gov/info/smallbus/qasbsec.htm

SEC Brochure *(Continued)*

Section 3(a)(11) of the Securities Act is generally known as the "intrastate offering exemption." This exemption facilitates the financing of local business operations. To qualify for the intrastate offering exemption, your company must:

- be incorporated in the state where it is offering the securities;
- carry out a significant amount of its business in that state; and
- make offers and sales only to residents of that state.

There is no fixed limit on the size of the offering or the number of purchasers. Your company must determine the residence of each purchaser. If any of the securities are offered or sold to even one out-of-state person, the exemption may be lost. Without the exemption, the company could be in violation of the Securities Act registration requirements. If a purchaser resells any of the securities to a person who resides outside the state within a short period of time after the company's offering is complete (the usual test is nine months), the entire transaction, including the original sales, might violate the Securities Act. Since secondary markets for these securities rarely develop, companies often must sell securities in these offerings at a discount.

It will be difficult for your company to rely on the intrastate exemption unless you know the purchasers and the sale is directly negotiated with them. If your company holds some of its assets outside the state, or derives a substantial portion of its revenues outside the state where it proposes to offer its securities, it will probably have a difficult time qualifying for the exemption.

You may follow Rule 147, a "safe harbor" rule, to ensure that you meet the requirements for this exemption. It is possible, however, that transactions not meeting all requirements of Rule 147 may still qualify for the exemption.

B. Private Offering Exemption

Section 4(2) of the Securities Act exempts from registration "transactions by an issuer not involvingany public offering." To qualify for this exemption, the purchasers of the securities must:

- have enough knowledge and experience in finance and business matters to evaluate the risks and merits of the investment (the "sophisticated investor"), or be able to bear the investment's economic risk;
- have access to the type of information normally provided in a prospectus; and
- agree not to resell or distribute the securities to the public.

In addition, you may not use any form of public solicitation or general advertising in connection with the offering.

The precise limits of this private offering exemption are uncertain. As the number of purchasers increases and their relationship to the company and its management becomes more remote, it is more difficult to show that the transaction qualifies for the exemption. You should know that if you offer securities to even one person who does not meet the necessary conditions, the entire offering may be in violation of the Securities Act.

http://www.sec.gov/info/smallbus/qasbsec.htm

SEC Brochure (*Continued*)

Rule 506, another "safe harbor" rule, provides objective standards that you can rely on to meet the requirements of this exemption. Rule 506 is a part of Regulation D, which we describe more fully on page 24.

C. Regulation A

Section 3(b) of the Securities Act authorizes the SEC to exempt from registration small securities offerings. By this authority, we created Regulation A, an exemption for public offerings not exceeding $5 million in any 12-month period. If you choose to rely on this exemption, your company must file an offering statement, consisting of a notification, offering circular, and exhibits, with the SEC for review.

Regulation A offerings share many characteristics with registered offerings. For example, you must provide purchasers with an offering circular that is similar in content to a prospectus. Like registered offerings, the securities can be offered publicly and are not "restricted," meaning they are freely tradeable in the secondary market after the offering. The principal advantages of Regulation A offerings, as opposed to full registration, are:

- The financial statements are simpler and don't need to be audited;
- There are no Exchange Act reporting obligations after the offering unless the company has more than $10 million in total assets and more than 500 shareholders;
- Companies may choose among three formats to prepare the offering circular, one of which is a simplified question-and-answer document; and
- You may "test the waters" to determine if there is adequate interest in your securities before going through the expense of filing with the SEC.

All types of companies which do not report under the Exchange Act may use Regulation A, except "blank check" companies, those with an unspecified business, and investment companies registered or required to be registered under the Investment Company Act of 1940. In most cases, shareholders may use Regulation A to resell up to $1.5 million of securities.

If you "test the waters," you can use general solicitation and advertising prior to filing an offering statement with the SEC, giving you the advantage of determining whether there is enough market interest in your securities before you incur the full range of legal, accounting, and other costs associated with filing an offering statement. You may not, however, solicit or accept money until the SEC staff completes its review of the filed offering statement and you deliver prescribed offering materials to investors.

D. Regulation D

Regulation D establishes three exemptions from Securities Act registration. Let's address each one separately.

Rule 504

Rule 504 provides an exemption for the offer and sale of up to $1,000,000 of securities in a 12-month period. Your company may use this exemption so long as it is not a blank check company and is not subject to Exchange Act reporting requirements. Like the other Regulation D exemptions, in

http://www.sec.gov/info/smallbus/qasbsec.htm

SEC Brochure (*Continued*)

general you may not use public solicitation or advertising to market the securities and purchasers receive "restricted" securities, meaning that they may not sell the securities without registration or an applicable exemption. However, you can use this exemption for a public offering of your securities and investors will receive freely tradable securities under the following circumstances:

- You register the offering exclusively in one or more states that require a publicly filed registration statement and delivery of a substantive disclosure document to investors;
- You register and sell in a state that requires registration and disclosure delivery and also sell in a state without those requirements, so long as you deliver the disclosure documents mandated by the state in which you registered to all purchasers; or,
- You sell exclusively according to state law exemptions that permit general solicitation and advertising, so long as you sell only to "accredited investors," a term we describe in more detail below in connection with Rule 505 and Rule 506 offerings.

Even if you make a private sale where there are no specific disclosure delivery requirements, you should take care to provide sufficient information to investors to avoid violating the antifraud provisions of the securities laws. This means that any information you provide to investors must be free from false or misleading statements. Similarly, you should not exclude any information if the omission makes what you do provide investors false or misleading.

Rule 505

Rule 505 provides an exemption for offers and sales of securities totaling up to $5 million in any 12-month period. Under this exemption, you may sell to an unlimited number of "accredited investors" and up to 35 other persons who do not need to satisfy the sophistication or wealth standards associated with other exemptions. Purchasers must buy for investment only, and not for resale. The issued securities are "restricted." Consequently, you must inform investors that they may not sell for at least a year without registering the transaction. You may not use general solicitation or advertising to sell the securities.

An "accredited investor" is:

- a bank, insurance company, registered investment company, business development company, or small business investment company;
- an employee benefit plan, within the meaning of the Employee Retirement Income Security Act, if a bank, insurance company, or registered investment adviser makes the investment decisions, or if the plan has total assets in excess of $5 million;
- a charitable organization, corporation or partnership with assets exceeding $5 million;
- a director, executive officer, or general partner of the company selling the securities;
- a business in which all the equity owners are accredited investors;
- a natural person with a net worth of at least $1 million;
- a natural person with income exceeding $200,000 in each of the two most recent years or joint income with a spouse exceeding $300,000 for those years and a reasonable expectation of the same income

http://www.sec.gov/info/smallbus/qasbsec.htm

SEC Brochure *(Continued)*

level in the current year; or

- a trust with assets of at least $5 million, not formed to acquire the securities offered, and whose purchases are directed by a sophisticated person.

It is up to you to decide what information you give to accredited investors, so long as it does not violate the antifraud prohibitions. But you must give non-accredited investors disclosure documents that generally are the same as those used in registered offerings. If you provide information to accredited investors, you must make this information available to the non-accredited investors as well. You must also be available to answer questions by prospective purchasers.

Here are some specifics about the financial statement requirements applicable to this type of offering:

- Financial statements need to be certified by an independent public accountant;
- If a company other than a limited partnership cannot obtain audited financial statements without unreasonable effort or expense, only the company's balance sheet, to be dated within 120 days of the start of the offering, must be audited, and
- Limited partnerships unable to obtain required financial statements without unreasonable effort or expense may furnish audited financial statements prepared under the federal income tax laws.

Rule 506

As we discussed earlier, Rule 506 is a "safe harbor" for the private offering exemption. If your company satisfies the following standards, you can be assured that you are within the Section 4(2) exemption:

- You can raise an unlimited amount of capital;
- You cannot use general solicitation or advertising to market the securities;
- You can sell securities to an unlimited number of accredited investors (the same group we identified in the Rule 505 discussion) and up to 35 other purchasers. Unlike Rule 505, all non-accredited investors, either alone or with a purchaser representative, must be sophisticated - that is, they must have sufficient knowledge and experience in financial and business matters to make them capable of evaluating the merits and risks of the prospective investment;
- It is up to you to decide what information you give to accredited investors, so long as it does not violate the antifraud prohibitions. But you must give non-accredited investors disclosure documents that generally are the same as those used in registered offerings. If you provide information to accredited investors, you must make this information available to the non-accredited investors as well;
- You must be available to answer questions by prospective purchasers;
- Financial statement requirements are the same as for Rule 505; and
- Purchasers receive "restricted" securities. Consequently, purchasers may not freely trade the securities in the secondary market after the offering.

E. Accredited Investor Exemption - Section 4(6)

http://www.sec.gov/info/smallbus/qasbsec.htm

SEC Brochure (*Continued*)

Section 4(6) of the Securities Act exempts from registration offers and sales of securities to accredited investors when the total offering price is less than $5 million.

The definition of accredited investors is the same as that used in Regulation D. Like the exemptions in Rule 505 and 506, this exemption does not permit any form of advertising or public solicitation. There are no document delivery requirements. Of course, all transactions are subject to the antifraud provisions of the securities laws.

F. California Limited Offering Exemption - Rule 1001

SEC Rule 1001 provides an exemption from the registration requirements of the Securities Act for offers and sales of securities, in amounts of up to $5 million, that satisfy the conditions of §25102(n) of the California Corporations Code. This California law exempts from California state law registration offerings made by California companies to "qualified purchasers" whose characteristics are similar to, but not the same as, accredited investors under Regulation D. This exemption allows some methods of general solicitation prior to sales.

G. Exemption for Sales of Securities through Employee Benefit Plans - Rule 701

The SEC's Rule 701 exempts sales of securities if made to compensate employees. This exemption is available only to companies that are not subject to Exchange Act reporting requirements. You can sell at least $1,000,000 of securities under this exemption, no matter how small your company is. You can sell even more if you satisfy certain formulas based on your company's assets or on the number of its outstanding securities. If you sell more than $5 million in securities in a 12-month period, you need to provide limited disclosure documents to your employees. Employees receive "restricted securities" in these transactions and may not freely offer or sell them to the public.

VII. Are There State Law Requirements in Addition to Federal Ones?

The federal government and state governments each have their own securities laws and regulations. If your company is selling securities, it must comply with federal and state securities laws. If a particular offering is exempt under the federal securities laws, that does not necessarily mean that it is exempt from any of the state laws.

Historically, most state legislatures have followed one of two approaches in regulating public offerings of securities, or a combination of the two approaches. Some states review small businesses' securities offerings to ensure that companies disclose to investors all information needed to make an informed investment decision. Other states also analyze public offerings using substantive standards to assure that the terms and structure of the offerings are fair to investors, in addition to the focus on disclosure.

To facilitate small business capital formation, the North American Securities Administrators Association, or NASAA, in conjunction with the American Bar Association, developed the Small Company Offering Registration, also

http://www.sec.gov/info/smallbus/qasbsec.htm

SEC Brochure (Continued)

known as SCOR. SCOR is a simplified "question and answer" registration form that companies also can use as the disclosure document for investors. SCOR was primarily designed for state registration of small business securities offerings conducted under the SEC's Rule 504, for sale of securities up to $1,000,000, discussed on page 20. Currently, over 45 states recognize SCOR. To assist small business issuers in completing the SCOR Form, NASAA has developed a detailed "Issuer's Manual." This manual is available through NASAA's Web site at http://www.nasaa.org.

In addition, a small company can use the SCOR Form, called Form U-7, to satisfy many of the filing requirements of the SEC's Regulation A exemption, for sales of securities of up to $5,000,000 (discussed on page 19), since the company may file it with the SEC as part of the Regulation A offering statement.

To assist small businesses offering in several states, many states coordinate SCOR or Regulation A filings through a program called regional review. Regional reviews are available in the New England, Mid-Atlantic, Midwest and Western regions.

Companies seeking additional information on SCOR, regional reviews or the "Issuer's Manual" should contact NASAA.

VIII. What Resources Are Available Through the U.S. Small Business Administration?

When assessing your capital needs, you should consider programs offered through the U.S. Small Business Administration (SBA). Congress established the SBA in 1953 to aid, counsel, and protect the interests of the Nation's small business community. The SBA accomplishes this in part by working with intermediaries, banks, and other lending institutions to provide loans and venture capital financing to small businesses unable to secure financing through normal lending channels. The SBA offers financing through the programs listed below.

7(a) Loan Guaranty Program:

This is the SBA's primary lending program and was designed to meet the majority of the small business lending community's financing needs. In addition to general financing, the 7(a) program also encompasses a number of specialized loan programs. The following are a few of the many specialized loan programs:

Low Doc

This program is designed to increase the availability of funds under $100,000 and streamline or expedite the loan review process.

CAPLines

An umbrella program to help small businesses meet their short-term and cyclical working-capital needs with five separate programs.

http://www.sec.gov/info/smallbus/qasbsec.htm

SEC Brochure (Continued)

International Trade

If your business is preparing to engage in or is already engaged in international trade, or is adversely affected by competition from imports, the International Trade Loan Program is for you; and

DELTA

Defense Loan and Technical Assistance is a joint SBA and Department of Defense effort to provide financial and technical assistance to defense-dependent small firms adversely affected by cutbacks in defense.

Microloan Program

This program works through intermediaries to provide small loans from as little as $100 up to $25,000.

Certified Development Company (504 Loan) Program

This program, commonly referred to as the 504 program, makes long term loans available for purchasing land, buildings, machinery and equipment, and for building, modernizing or renovating existing facilities and sites.

Small Business Investment Company Program

Small Business Investment Companies (SBICs), which the SBA licenses and regulates, are privately-owned and managed investment firms that provide venture capital and start-up financing to small businesses.

To find additional information on these and other financial programs please contact your local SBA District Office (call 1-800-8-ASK-SBA for the nearest office) or look on SBA's Web site (http://www.sba.gov).

Additional Financial Resources and Information from the SBA's Office of Advocacy

Angel Capital Electronic Network (ACE-Net)

The Office of Advocacy of SBA has established an Internet site where small companies may list their Regulation A and Regulation D 504/SCOR stock offerings. ACE-Net is a cooperative effort between SBA and nine universities, state-based entities, and other non-profit organizations to provide a listing service where small companies may list their stock offering for review by high net worth investors (accredited investors). In addition, ACE-Net anticipates providing mentoring and educational services for small companies needing business planning and securities information. You can find the ACE-Net Internet site at the following URLs: http://www.sba.gov/ADVO/ or http://www.ace-net.org.

Small Business Lending in the United States

The Office of Advocacy of SBA has ranked the nearly 10,000 banks in the country on a state-by-state basis to determine which banks are "small business friendly." The state-by-state directory helps small businesses locate which banks in their area are more likely to lend to small business. The directory is available over the Internet at:

http://www.sec.gov/info/smallbus/qasbsec.htm

SEC Brochure (Continued)

http://www.sba.gov/ADVO/stats/.

IX. Where Can I Go for More Information?

The staff of the SEC's Office of Small Business and the SEC's Small Business Ombudsman will be glad to assist you with any questions you may have regarding federal securities laws. For information about state securities laws, contact NASAA or your state's securities administrator, whose office is usually located in your capital city.

The entire text of the SEC's rules and regulations is available through the U.S. Government Printing Office or from several private publishers of legal information. In addition, numerous books on this subject have been published, and some are available at public libraries. As of this writing, the following volumes of Title 17 of the Code of Federal Regulations (the SEC's rules and regulations) were available from the Government Printing Office:

- Vol. II - Parts 200 to 239. SEC Organization; Conduct and Ethics; Information and Requests; Rules of Practice; Regulation S-X and Securities Act of 1933.
- Vol III - Parts 240 to End. Securities Exchange Act of 1934; Public Utility Holding Company, Trust Indenture, Investment Company, Investment Advisers, and Securities Investor Protection Corporation Acts.

For additional information about how to obtain official publications of Commission rules and regulations, contact:

Superintendent of Documents
Government Printing Office
Washington DC 20402-9325

For copies of SEC forms and recent SEC releases:

Publications Section
U.S. Securities and Exchange Commission
450 Fifth Street N.W.
Washington, D.C. 20549-0019
Telephone: (202)942-4046

Other useful addresses, telephone numbers, web sites and e-mail:

SEC's World Wide Web site: http://www.sec.gov

SEC Office of Small Business
SEC Small Business Ombudsman
U.S. Securities and Exchange Commission
450 Fifth Street, N.W.
Washington, D.C. 20549-0304
Telephone: (202) 942-2950

E-mail addresses:
smallbusiness@sec.gov

http://www.sec.gov/info/smallbus/qasbsec.htm

SEC Brochure (*Continued*)

help@sec.gov

North American Securities Administrators Association
10 "G" Street, N.E., Suite 710
Washington, D.C. 20002
(202) 737-0900

NASAA's World Wide Web site: http://www.nasaa.org

SBA's World Wide Web site: http://www.sba.gov

ACE-Net World Wide Web site: http://www.ace-net.org

X. How Can We Improve this Guide?

If you have any suggestions about how we can make this booklet more useful, please contact the SEC staff at the mailing address, phone number or e-mail address noted above.

http://www.sec.gov/info/smallbus/qasbsec.htm

http://www.sec.gov/info/smallbus/qasbsec.htm

SEC Brochure (Continued)

Active Capital—Frequently Asked Questions

What Is Active Capital?

Active Capital is the simple, secure, and low-cost way for investors and small companies to find each other. It is an Internet-based listing service for securities offerings of small, growing companies located throughout the nation, that are viewed anonymously by accredited investors.

Who Needs Active Capital?

Entrepreneurs with small, growing businesses can use Active Capital to attract equity investors while meeting the legal requirements of federal and state securities regulators.

Venture capitalists, institutional investors, and individual accredited investors can use Active Capital to find investment opportunities from across the nation.

Who Manages Active Capital?

Overall management is provided by Phil Borden, Ph.D., and Jay Delong. Both have established reputations in high-technology venturing, leading nonprofit organizations, incubation, investment, and economic development. You may contact them at:

www.activecapital.org
877/ANGEL79 (877/234-3579)
18662 MacArthur Blvd., Suite 200, Irvine, CA 92612

Reprinted with permission from Active Capital.

Regional nonprofit, university-based, or state-based entrepreneurial development centers called "network operators" manage day-to-day operations that affect entrepreneurs. Network operators are established leaders in all aspects of economic development in their regions.

How Is Active Capital Different from Other Internet-Based Investment Programs?

Active Capital operates under the guidance of a no-action letter issued by the SEC. The letter requires that all small companies listed on Active Capital be "in full compliance with the appropriate filing and registration requirements of federal and state securities laws and regulations."

Active Capital has also consulted with the North American Securities Administrators Association, Inc. (NASAA), the national organization devoted to investor protection and made up of every state securities regulator. NASAA has cleared Active Capital's listings.

In short, once Active Capital has accepted a business plan into its database, and presuming the information in the plan is accurate, it already has cleared all regulatory hurdles in almost every state.

Active Capital is a not-for-profit listing service that is designed to facilitate the flow of information between entrepreneurs and investors. It is not designed to be a source of clients or business for attorneys, consultants, brokers, dealers, or any others who charge fees for services to entrepreneurs or investors.

Active Capital is not a broker-dealer, an investment adviser, or a securities exchange, and therefore, there are no "success fees" or commissions.

Active Capital charges a nominal fee to cover its administrative costs, but this fee is in no way contingent or related in any manner to the outcome or completion of any transaction resulting from a company's listing on Active Capital.

Can Any Investor Enroll with Active Capital?

Only "accredited" investors may enroll with Active Capital.

The SEC defines an individual accredited investor as a person with over $1 million in assets or whose income is at least $200,000 ($300,000 jointly with a spouse).

The SEC defines an institutional accredited investor to include several types of financial institutions such as bank, broker, dealer, insurance company, investment company, or Small Business Investment Corporation (SBIC).

The Active Capital Investor Application requires investors to certify that they meet these criteria.

Can Any Entrepreneur Enroll with Active Capital?

Only entrepreneurs who can sell security interest in their companies can enroll with Active Capital.

This means corporations and limited liability companies (LLCs) may be listed on the Active Capital company database.

The following business entities cannot list on Active Capital: sole proprietorships, general or limited partnerships, joint ventures, "blank check" or development stage companies, or those involved in oil, gas, or other extractive interests.

The Active Capital Entrepreneur Application requires entrepreneurs to certify that their companies meet the organizational criteria.

How Much Does It Cost to Enroll with Active Capital?

Active Capital is a fee-based service. Until June 2005, enrollment will be free to the entrepreneur. After June, the maximum annual fee will be $1,000. Enrollment provides both the investor and entrepreneur with unlimited access to all Active Capital educational, listing, and support services.

In addition to the Active Capital fee, most network operators are funded by states that compensate the fee for in-state investors or entrepreneurs. They may charge no fees or greatly reduced fees. Others may charge entrepreneurs for specific services. The choice of paying for such services or seeking other support is up to each entrepreneur.

Check with the local network operator for more information on fees and other services they may offer to the investor-entrepreneur community.

How Do Active Capital Fees Compare to "Go It Alone" Costs?

Active Capital is far less expensive. The single fee provides a registration exemption in almost every state and with the SEC. Going it alone and staying in compliance with federal and state regulations requires registering in each state in which an offer will be made, plus such other fees as attorneys, broker-dealers, and others may assess for the registration process.

Such fees routinely cost $15,000 to $30,000 per state, though it may vary according to the attorney, state, or other expert. It is wise to have an attorney or other expert look over an Active Capital filing, but that review typically will be less than $2,000 and may not be necessary at all. Entrepreneurs should consult their local attorneys and experts to verify the specific information for each specific case.

How Much Capital Can Be Raised Using Active Capital?

A small, growing company can raise up to $5 million using Active Capital. However, Active Capital is especially helpful for companies seeking up to $1 million in financing.

Entrepreneurs can raise up to $1 million without having to register their securities offering under the SEC's Regulation D, Rule 504, and by taking advantage of the Model Accredited Investor Exemption or similar state variation that have been adopted by a majority of states.

Entrepreneurs can also raise up to $1 million under the SEC's Regulation D, Rule 504, by listing their securities offering registered with states.

Entrepreneurs can also raise up to $5 million under the SEC's Regulation A, by listing their securities offering registered with states.

How Much Does Active Capital Itself Lend or Invest?

Nothing. Active Capital is not a lender or investor. It works with entrepreneurs and investors to voluntarily link both, so that they may work with each other.

Do I Need a Lawyer to List on Active Capital?

Offering corporate securities for sale involves significant responsibilities under both federal and state securities laws. Therefore, while most of the documents required for listing on Active Capital can be prepared on your own, Active Capital strongly encourages you to seek qualified legal professional assistance during every stage of securities offering.

Prior to listing on Active Capital, you are also urged to work with an attorney to develop a comprehensive securities law compliance plan specific to your proposed offering.

It is critical that you comply with all legal requirements as any mistake you make will not only lead to serious liability, but can also affect your ability to obtain further equity financing later.

If I Fill Out My Form but Do Not Post It Right Away, Do I Need to Sign Up Again?

Your registration is good for one year. You do not have to reregister within that year. It typically takes several sessions to complete the U-7. It is in your best interest to complete it early, in order to give yourself the most chances to be "seen."

After I Have Filled Out All My Forms, May I Change My Answers?

Yes. Companies evolve, projections change, and counselors and investors make suggestions worth considering. You may change your profile as often as you like. However, each time you do, you must sign, date, and submit a new hard copy.

This process protects both investors and entrepreneurs. It protects investors by making certain that the plan that may lead to an offer has not changed without notice, and it protects both parties from lawsuits about the accuracy of the information in a particular offering.

Must I Notify Active Capital After I Have Made a Deal?

No, but we'd sure love it. SEC regulations keep us from advertising the success stories of individual companies, but we aggregate the data in order to know what we can do better and how to design more effective help.

Can I Use Active Capital If I Am a Canadian or Other Non-U.S. Company?

At present Active Capital works only with U.S. companies, because all of its securities regulations clearances are U.S. based. However, if a non-U.S. company wishes to list for purposes of seeking investors but understands that it has none of the "safe harbors" listed above, it may do so.

Can I Get Other Forms of Non-Equity Financing through Active Capital?

No. Active Capital listings all rest on investors taking an equity (ownership) position in the company.

However, Active Capital is working on relationships with non-equity capital providers (e.g., term loans, revolving loans, leases, insurance providers, etc.). Watch the site for links.

How Do I Learn When Potential Investors Read My Plan?

When the investor contacts you. One of the values of Active Capital is the security we provide both investors and entrepreneurs.

While we cannot provide you with a detailed list of investors who have seen your plan, your Local Operator can let you know how many hits your plan has received monthly. It will be a rough guide to the degree of interest in your company.

How Many Investors May Review My Plan?

Up to the total number in the investor database. Of course, it is unreasonable to think every investor will be interested. Investors' interests will be dictated by the field of interest of the company, the type of business it is, the region of the country in which it is located, the maturity of the company, the experience of the CEO, and so on. Although angel investors typically like to invest early in the evolution of a company, an investor may take an interest in any level of maturity or business type. It is impossible to predict what will turn on a particular investor.

Therefore, the Active Capital database creates a company profile based on each answer within the U-7. Each answer is searchable by investors. Investors look for matches with their interests, then pursue them as they please.

Do All Investors Demand to Play a Role in Each Company?

A "qualified no." Angels like to be active investors. However, each situation is different. How active an angel will be depends on both what the investor is looking for and the level of maturity of the company.

If the company has a management or marketing or other weakness in which the angel can offer experience, the angel may do so on a voluntary basis or as a condition of the investment. If the angel is interested only in return, the angel may take a very light role. One thing an entrepreneur can count on is that any investor will do very careful due diligence before investing and will create investment and active management strategies based on what is discovered.

How Can Lawyers or Accountants or Consultants Register on Active Capital?

They cannot register as an entity. Active Capital is not designed as a source of business for them. Only companies and investors may register on Active Capital. If a registering company chooses to have an attorney or accountant or consultant act on its behalf, it may do so by having the outside expert sign off on the submission form.

If an attorney or accountant or consultant wishes to register as an accredited investor, or as a local operator, Active Capital will investigate their application and act accordingly.

Can I Register on Active Capital if I Have Filed for a Public Stock Offering with the SEC or Have Not "Blue Skyed" in Every State in Which I Am Seeking Investment?

Yes to both questions. The whole idea of Active Capital is to save you the separate filing fees in the various states. We take care of "blue skying" for you. If the states in which you file subscribe to the Model Accredited Investor Exemption (MAIE), which our original company, ACE-Net, helped to develop, then a single filing on Active Capital exempts you from state filing fees; 48 states either subscribe to MAIE or have laws that harmonize with it while not using it specifically.

State Securities Regulations Administrators

Alabama
Securities Commission
770 Washington Avenue, Suite 570
Montgomery, AL 36130-4700
(334) 242-2984

Alaska
Department of Community &
  Economic Development
Division of Banking, Securities &
  Corporations
P.O. Box 110807
Juneau, AK 99811-0807
(907) 465-2521

Arizona
Corporation Commission
Securities Division
1300 West Washington Street,
  3rd Floor
Phoenix, AZ 85007
(602) 542-4242

Arkansas
Securities Department
Heritage West Building
201 East Markham, Room 300
Little Rock, AR 72201
(501) 324-9260

California
Department of Corporations
1515 K Street, Suite 200
Sacramento, CA 95814
(916) 445-7205

Colorado
Division of Securities
1580 Lincoln Street, Suite 420
Denver, CO 80203
(303) 894-2320

Connecticut
Department of Banking
260 Constitution Place
Hartford, CT 06103-1800
(860) 240-8230

Delaware
Department of Justice
Division of Securities
Carvel State Office Building
820 North French Street, 5th Floor
Wilmington, DE 19801
(302) 577-8424

District of Columbia
Department of Insurance,
    Securities, and Banking
810 First Street, NE, Suite 701
Washington, DC 20002
(202) 727-8000

Florida
Office of Financial Regulation
200 East Gaines Street
The Fletcher Building
Tallahassee, FL 32399-0372
(850) 410-9805

Georgia
Office of the Secretary of State
Securities and Business
    Regulation Division
Two Martin Luther King Jr. Drive
    SE
802 West Tower
Atlanta, GA 30334
(404) 656-3920

Hawaii
Department of Commerce &
    Consumer Affairs
1010 Richards Street, 2nd Floor
Honolulu, HI 96813
(808) 586-2744

Idaho
Department of Finance
700 West State Street, 2nd Floor
Boise, ID 83720
(208) 332-8000

Illinois
Office of the Secretary of State
Securities Department
69 West Washington Street,
    Suite 1220
Chicago, IL 60602
(217) 782-2256

Indiana
Office of the Secretary of State
Securities Division
302 West Washington,
    Room E-111
Indianapolis, IN 46204
(317) 232-6681

Iowa
Insurance Division
Securities Bureau
330 Maple Street
Des Moines, IA 50319-0065
(515) 281-5705

Kansas

Office of the Securities
  Commissioner
618 South Kansas Avenue
Topeka, KS 66603-3804
(785) 296-3307

Kentucky

Department of Financial
  Institutions
1025 Capital Center Drive,
  Suite 200
Frankfort, KY 40601
(502) 573-3390

Louisiana

Securities Commission
Office of Financial Institutions
8660 United Plaza Boulevard,
  2nd Floor
Baton Rouge, LA 70809-7024

Maine

Securities Division
State House Station 121
Augusta, ME 04333
(207) 624-8551

Maryland

Office of the Attorney General
Division of Securities
200 Saint Paul Place
Baltimore, MD 21202-2020
(410) 576-6360

Massachusetts

Securities Division
One Ashburton Place, Room 1701
Boston, MA 02108
(617) 727-3548

Michigan

Securities Division
Office of Financial & Insurance
  Services
Department of Labor & Economic
  Growth
611 West Ottawa Street
Lansing, MI 48933
(877) 999-6442

Minnesota

Department of Commerce
85 East 7th Place, Suite 500
Saint Paul, MN 55101
(651) 296-4973

Mississippi
Office of the Secretary of State
Business Regulation &
    Enforcement Division
700 North Street
Jackson, MS 39202
(601) 359-2663

Missouri
Office of the Secretary of State
600 West Main Street
Jefferson City, MO 65101
(573) 751-4136

Montana
Office of the State Auditor
Securities Department
840 Helena Avenue
Helena, MT 59601
(406) 444-2040

Nebraska
Department of Banking & Finance
Bureau of Securities
1200 N Street, Suite 311
Lincoln, NE 68508
(402) 471-3445

Nevada
Secretary of State
Securities Division
555 East Washington Avenue
5th Floor, Suite 5200
Las Vegas, NV 89101
(702) 486-2440

New Hampshire
Bureau of Securities Regulation
State House Annex
Suite 317A, 3rd Floor
Concord, NH 03301
(603) 271-1463

New Jersey
Department of Law & Public
    Safety
Bureau of Securities
153 Halsey Street, 6th Floor
Newark, NJ 07102
(973) 504-3600

New Mexico
Regulation & Licensing
    Department
Securities Division
725 St. Michaels Drive
Santa Fe, NM 87505
(505) 827-7140

New York

Office of the Attorney General
Investor Protection & Securities
  Bureau
120 Broadway, 23rd Floor
New York, NY 10271
(212) 416-8200

North Carolina

Department of the Secretary of
  State
Securities Division
P.O. Box 29622
Raleigh, NC 27626-0622
(919) 733-3924

North Dakota

Securities Commission
600 East Boulevard
State Capitol, 5th Floor
Bismarck, ND 58505-0510
(701) 328-2910

Ohio

Division of Securities
77 South High Street,
  22nd Floor
Columbus, OH 43215
(614) 644-7381

Oklahoma

Department of Securities
1st National Center, Suite 860
120 North Robinson
Oklahoma City, OK 73102
(405) 280-7700

Oregon

Department of Consumer &
  Business Services
Division of Finance &
  Corporation Securities
350 Winter Street, NE, Room 410
Salem, OR 97301-3881
(503) 378-4387

Pennsylvania

Securities Commission
Eastgate Office Building
1010 North 7th Street, 2nd Floor
Harrisburg, PA 17102-1410
(717) 787-8061

Puerto Rico

Commission of Financial
  Institutions
1492 Ponce de Leon Avenue,
  Suite 600
San Juan, PR 00907
(787) 723-3131 ext. 2222

Rhode Island
Department of Business
  Regulation
233 Richmond Street, Suite 232
Providence, RI 02903-4232
(401) 222-3048

South Carolina
Office of the Attorney General
Securities Division
Rembert C. Dennis Office
  Building
1000 Assembly Street
Columbia, SC 29201
(803) 734-4731

South Dakota
Division of Securities
445 East Capitol Avenue
Pierre, SD 57501-2000
(605) 773-4823

Tennessee
Department of Commerce &
  Insurance
Securities Division
Davy Crockett Tower, Suite 680
500 James Robertson Parkway
Nashville, TN 37243-0575
(615) 741-2947

Texas
State Securities Board
208 East 10th Street, 5th Floor
Austin, TX 78701
(512) 305-8300

Utah
Department of Commerce
Division of Securities
160 East 300 South, 2nd Floor
Salt Lake City, UT 84111
(801) 530-6600

Vermont
Department of Banking Insurance
Securities & Health Care
  Administration
89 Main Street, Drawer 20
Montpelier, VT 05620-3101
(802) 828-3420

Virginia
State Corporation Commission
Division of Securities & Retail
  Franchising
1300 East Main Street, 9th Floor
Richmond, VA 23219
(804) 371-9051

Washington

Department of Financial
   Institutions
Securities Division
P.O. Box 41200
Olympia, WA 98504-1200
(360) 902-8700

West Virginia

West Virginia State Auditor's
   Office
Securities Division
State Capitol Building 1,
   Room W-100
Charleston, WV 25305-0230
(304) 558-2257

Wisconsin

Department of Financial
   Institutions
Division of Securities
345 West Washington Avenue,
   4th Floor
Madison, WI 53703
(608) 266-1064

Wyoming

Secretary of State
Securities Division
State Capitol, Room 109
200 West 24th Street
Cheyenne, WY 82002-0020
(307) 777-7370

Small Business Administration Loan Programs

As discussed in Chapter 3, most SBA loan programs involve commercial lenders as the source of funds, which leaves the SBA in the role of guaranteeing a percentage of the loans rather than making direct loans. Unless you are economically disadvantaged or the business is in a disadvantaged neighborhood, you will probably find your loan application will be processed under the SBA 7(a) program.

The SBA maintains a busy Web site at http://www.sba.gov, from which you can quickly become overloaded with information. To help you peruse the pertinent basic information, we have reprinted only the information that pertains to the SBA 7(a) program. Once you have digested what is here, you should find it easier to navigate the Web site to find any special programs that may fit your circumstances. (Also, since these special programs are frequently modified, it is a good idea to obtain the information from the Web site.)

Basic 7(a) Loan Program

The 7(a) loans are the most used type loan of the SBA's business loan programs. Its name comes from section 7(a) of the Small Business Act, which authorizes the Agency to provide business loans to American small businesses.

All 7(a) loans are provided by lenders who are called participants because they participate with the SBA in the 7(a) program. Not all lenders choose to participate, but most American banks do. There are also some non-bank lenders who participate with the SBA in the 7(a) program which expands the availability of lenders making loans under SBA guidelines.

The 7(a) loans are only available on a guaranty basis. This means they are provided by lenders who choose to structure their own loans by the SBA's requirements and who apply and receive a guaranty from the SBA on a portion of this loan. The SBA does not fully guaranty 7(a) loans. The lender and the SBA share the risk that a borrower will not be able to repay the loan in full. The guaranty is a guaranty against payment default. It does not cover imprudent decisions by the lender or misrepresentation by the borrower.

Under the guaranty concept, commercial lenders make and administer the loans. The business applies to a lender for their financing. The lender decides if they will make the loan internally or if the application has some weaknesses which, in their opinion, will require an SBA guaranty if the loan is to be made. The guaranty which the SBA provides is only available to the lender. It assures the lender that in the event the borrower does not repay their obligation and a payment default occurs, the government will reimburse the lender for its loss, up to the percentage of the

SBA's guaranty. Under this program, the borrower remains obligated for the full amount due.

All 7(a) loans which the SBA guaranty must meet 7(a) criteria. The business gets a loan from its lender with a 7(a) structure and the lender gets an SBA guaranty on a portion or percentage of this loan. Hence the primary business loan assistance program available to small businesses from the SBA is called the 7(a) guaranty loan program.

A key concept of the 7(a) guaranty loan program is that the loan actually comes from a commercial lender, not the government. If the lender is not willing to provide the loan, even if they may be able to get an SBA guaranty, the Agency cannot force the lender to change their mind. Neither can the SBA make the loan by itself because the Agency does not have any money to lend. Therefore it is paramount that all applicants positively approach the lender for a loan, and that they know the lender's criteria and requirements as well as those of the SBA. In order to obtain positive consideration for an SBA-supported loan, the applicant must be both eligible and creditworthy.

What SBA Seeks in a Loan Application

In order to get a 7(a) loan, the applicant must first be eligible. Repayment ability from the cash flow of the business is a primary consideration in the SBA loan decision process, but good character, management capability, collateral, and owner's equity contribution are also important considerations. All owners of 20 percent or more are required to personally guarantee SBA loans.

Eligibility Criteria

All applicants must be eligible to be considered for a 7(a) loan. The eligibility requirements are designed to be as broad as possible in order that this lending program can accommodate the most diverse variety of small business financing needs. All businesses that are considered for financing under the SBA 7(a) loan program must: meet SBA size standards, be for-profit, not already have the internal resources (business or personal) to provide the financing, and be able to demonstrate repayment. Certain variations of the SBA 7(a) loan program may also require additional eligibility criteria. Special purpose programs will identify those additional criteria.

Eligibility factors for all 7(a) loans include: size, type of business, use of proceeds, and the availability of funds from other sources. The following [pages] will provide more detailed information on these eligibility issues.

Small Business Size Standards

A Small Business is one that:

- is organized for profit;
- has a place of business in the United States;
- makes a significant contribution to the U.S. economy by paying taxes or using American products, materials or labor; and,
- does not exceed the numerical size standard for its industry.

The business may be a sole proprietorship, partnership, corporation, or any other legal form.

There is an SBA small business size standard for every private sector industry in the U.S. economy. SBA uses the North American Industry Classification System (NAIAS) to identify the industries.

Size Standards (usually stated in number of employees or average annual receipts) represent the largest size that a business (including its subsidiaries and affiliates) may be to remain classified as a small business for the SBA's programs and for federal contracting programs.

The SBA has several general size standards. A business in one of the following industry groups is small if it is not greater than the size standard indicated in the following table.

Industry Group	*Size Standard*
Manufacturing	500 employees
Wholesale Trade	100 employees
Agriculture	$750,000
Retail trade	$6 million
General & Heavy Construction (except Dredging)	$28.5 million
Dredging	$17 million
Special Trade Contractors	$12 million
Travel Agencies	$3 million

Industry Group (Continued)	*Size Standard (Continued)*
Business and Personal Services *Except:*	$6 million
1. Architectural, Engineering, Surveying, and Mapping Services	$4 million
2. Dry Cleaning and Carpet Cleaning Services	$4 million

If the size of a business exceeds the size standard for its overall industry group, it may still be a small business for the specific NAIAS industry in that group. Some industries have higher size standards than the general one for the industry group. The SBA has a table of size standards on its Web site.

Don't know the NAIAS code? Try the SBA's Search Routine on its Web site. Or you may search for NAIAS industries on the U.S. Bureau of the Census Web site.

For federal contracting, a small business must not exceed the size standard stated in the solicitation. The contracting officer designates the size standard of the procurement by selecting the size standard established for the NAIAS industry that best describes the principal purpose of the procurement.

Need more information on size standards? Please read the Small Business Size Regulations or our "Guide to the SBA's Definitions of Size Standards." For further information, you may write or call the Office of Size Standards.

Office of Size Standards
U.S. Small Business Administration
409 3rd St., SW
Washington, DC 20416
Phone: (202) 205-6618
Fax: (202) 205-6390
E-mail: sizestandards@sba.com

Eligible Businesses

The vast majority of businesses are eligible for financial assistance from the SBA. However, applicant businesses must operate for profit; be engaged in, or propose to do business in, the United States or its possessions; have reasonable owner equity to invest; and, use alternative financial resources first, including personal assets. It should be noted that some businesses are ineligible for financial assistance.

Certain other considerations apply to the types of businesses and applicants eligible for SBA loan programs.

BUSINESS TYPES AND APPLICANTS WITH ADDITIONAL CONSIDERATIONS

Franchises—are eligible except in situations where a franchisor retains power to control operations to such an extent as to be tantamount to an employment contract. The franchisee must have the right to profit from efforts commensurate with ownership.

Recreational facilities and clubs—are eligible provided: (a) the facilities are open to the general public, or (b) in membership-only situations, membership is not selectively denied to any particular group of individuals and the number of memberships is not restricted either as a whole or by establishing maximum limits for particular groups.

Farms and agricultural businesses—are eligible; however, these applicants should first explore the Farm Service Agency (FSA) programs, particularly if the applicant has a prior or existing relationship with the FSA.

Fishing vessels—are eligible; however, those seeking funds for the construction or reconditioning of vessels with a cargo capacity of five tons or more must first request financing from the National Marine Fisheries Service (NMFS), a part of the Department of Commerce.

Medical facilities—hospitals, clinics, emergency outpatient facilities, and medical and dental laboratories are eligible. Convalescent and nursing homes are eligible, provided they are licensed by the appropriate government agency and services rendered go beyond those of room and board.

An Eligible Passive Company (EPC) is a small entity which does not engage in regular and continuous business activity. An EPC must use loan proceeds to acquire or lease, and/or improve or renovate real or personal property that it leases to one or more Operating Companies for conducting the Operating Company's business. The EPC must comply with the conditions set forth in 13 CFR Sec. 120.111.

Change of ownership—Loans for this purpose are eligible provided the business benefits from the change. In most cases, this benefit should be seen in promoting the sound development of the business or, perhaps, in preserving its existence. Loans cannot be made when proceeds would enable a borrower to purchase: (a) part of a business in which it has no present interest or (b) part of an interest of a present and continuing owner. Loans to effect a change of ownership among members of the same family are discouraged.

Aliens—are eligible; however, consideration is given to the type of status possessed, e.g., resident, lawful temporary resident, etc., in determining the degree of risk relating to the continuity of the applicant's business. Excessive risk may be offset by full collateralization. The various types of visas may be discussed in more detail with the local SBA office.

Probation or parole—applications will not be accepted from firms where a principal (any one of those required to submit a personal history statement, SBA Form 912):

1. is currently incarcerated, on parole, or on probation;
2. is a defendant in a criminal proceeding; or
3. whose probation or parole is lifted expressly because it prohibits an SBA loan.

This restriction would not necessarily preclude a loan to a business, where a principal had responded in the affirmative to any one of the questions on the Statement of Personal History. These judgments are made on a case-by-case evaluation of the nature, frequency, and timing of the offenses. Fingerprint cards (available from the local SBA office) are required any time a question on the form is answered in the affirmative.

Ineligible Businesses

Businesses cannot be engaged in illegal activities, loan packaging, specu-
lation, multisales distribution, gambling, investment or lending, or where
the owner is on parole. Specific types of businesses not eligible include:

Real estate investment firms exist when the real property will be held for
investment purposes—as opposed to loans to otherwise eligible small
business concerns for the purpose of occupying the real estate being acquired.

Other speculative activities are those firms developing profits from fluc-
tuations in price rather than through the normal course of trade, such as
wildcatting for oil and dealing in commodities futures, when not part of
the regular activities of the business. Dealers of rare coins and stamps are
not eligible.

Lending activities include banks, finance companies, factors, leasing
companies, insurance companies (not agents), and any other firm whose
stock in trade is money.

Pyramid sales plans are characterized by endless chains of distributors
and sub-distributors where a participant's primary incentive is based on
the sales made by an ever-increasing number of participants. Such products as cosmetics, household goods, and other soft goods lend themselves
to this type of business.

Illegal activities are by definition those activities which are against the
law in the jurisdiction where the business is located. Included in these

activities are the production, servicing, or distribution of otherwise legal products that are to be used in connection with an illegal activity, such as selling drug paraphernalia or operating a motel that permits illegal prostitution.

Gambling activities include any business whose principal activity is gambling. While this precludes loans to race tracks, casinos, and similar enterprises, the rule does not restrict loans to otherwise eligible businesses, which obtain less than one-third of their annual gross income from either: 1) the sale of official state lottery tickets under a state license, or 2) legal gambling activities licensed and supervised by a state authority.

Charitable, religious, or other non-profit or eleemosynary institutions, government-owned corporations, consumer and marketing cooperatives, and churches and organizations promoting religious objectives are not eligible.

Use of Proceeds

7(a) loan proceeds may be used to establish a new business or to assist in the operation, acquisition or expansion of an existing business. These may include (non-exclusive):

1. To purchase land or buildings, to cover new construction as well as expansion or conversion of existing facilities;
2. To acquire equipment, machinery, furniture, fixtures, supplies, or materials;

3. For long-term working capital including the payment of accounts payable and/or for the purchase of inventory;

4. To refinance existing business indebtedness which is not already structured with reasonable terms and conditions;

5. For short-term working capital needs including: seasonal financing, contract performance, construction financing, export production, and for financing against existing inventory and receivable under special conditions; or

6. To purchase an existing business.

Ineligible Use of Proceeds

There are certain restrictions for the use of SBA loans. The following is a list of purposes which SBA loans cannot finance:

1. To refinance existing debt where the lender is in a position to sustain a loss and the SBA would take over that loss through refinancing;

2. To effect a partial change of business ownership or a change that will not benefit the business;

3. To permit the reimbursements of funds owed to any owner. This includes any equity injection, or injection of capital for the purposes of the business's continuance until the loan supported by the SBA is disbursed;

4. To repay delinquent state or federal withholding taxes or other funds that should be held in trust or escrow; and

5. For a nonsound business purpose.

Availability of Funds from Other Sources

The federal government does not extend credit to businesses where the financial strength of the individual owners or the company itself is sufficient to provide all or part of the financing. Therefore, the utilization of both the business and personal financial resources is reviewed as part of the eligibility criteria. If business and personal resources are found to be excessive, the business will be required to use those resources in lieu of part or all of the requested loan proceeds.

Character Considerations

The SBA must determine if the principals of each applicant firm have historically shown the willingness and ability to pay their debts and whether they abided by the laws of their community. The Agency must know if there are any factors which impact these issues. Therefore, a "Statement of Personal History" is obtained from each principal.

Other Aspects of the Basic 7(a) Loan Program

In addition to credit and eligibility criteria, an applicant should be aware of the general types of terms and conditions they can expect if the SBA is involved in the financial assistance. The specific terms of SBA loans are negotiated between an applicant and the participating financial institution, subject to the requirements of the SBA. In general, the following provisions apply to all SBA 7(a) loans. However, certain Loan Programs or Lender Programs vary from these standards. These variations are indicated for each program.

Maximum Loan Amounts (Updated as of 10/1/2004)

The SBA's 7(a) Loan Program has a maximum loan amount of $2 million. The SBA's maximum exposure is $1.0 million. Thus, if a business receives an SBA-guaranteed loan for $2 million, the maximum guaranty to the lender will be $1.0 million or 50 percent.

Interest Rates Applicable to SBA 7(a) Loans

Interest rates are negotiated between the borrower and the lender but are subject to SBA maximums, which are pegged to the Prime Rate.

Interest rates may be fixed or variable. Fixed rate loans of $50,000 or more must not exceed Prime Plus 2.25 percent if the maturity is less than 7 years, and Prime Plus 2.75 percent if the maturity is 7 years or more.

For loans between $25,000 and $50,000, maximum rates must not exceed Prime Plus 3.25 percent if the maturity is less than 7 years, and Prime Plus 3.75 percent if the maturity is 7 years or more.

For loans of $25,000 or less, the maximum interest rate must not exceed Prime Plus 4.25 percent if the maturity is less than 7 years, and Prime Plus 4.75 percent, if the maturity is 7 years or more.

Variable rate loans may be pegged to either the lowest prime rate or the SBA optional peg rate. The optional peg rate is a weighted average of rates the federal government pays for loans with maturities similar to the average SBA loan. It is calculated quarterly and published in the "Federal Register." The lender and the borrower negotiate the amount of the spread which will be added to the base rate. An adjustment period is selected which will identify the frequency at which the note rate will change. It must be no more often than monthly and must be consistent (e.g., monthly, quarterly, semiannually, annually or any other defined, consistent period).

Percentage of Guaranty on 7(a) Loans

For those applicants that meet the SBA's credit and eligibility standards, the Agency can guaranty up to 85 percent of loans of $150,000 and less, and up to 75 percent of loans above $150,000. This standard applies to most variations of the 7(a) Loan Program. However, SBA Express loans carry a maximum guaranty of 50 percent guaranty. The Export Working Capital Loan Program carries a maximum of 90 percent guaranty, up to a guaranteed amount of $1 million.

SBA Fees for 7(a) Loans

Fees Associated with SBA Loans

To offset the costs of the SBA's loan programs to the taxpayer, the Agency charges lenders a guaranty and a servicing fee for each loan approved. These fees can be passed on to the borrower once they have been paid by the lender. The amount of the fees are determined by the amount of the loan guaranty.

For loans approved on or after October 1, 2004, the following fee structure applies:

> For loans of $150,000 or less, a 2 percent guaranty fee will be charged. Lenders are again permitted to retain 25 percent of the up-front guarantee fee on loans with a gross amount of $150,000 or less.
>
> For loans more than $150,000 but up to and including $700,000, a 3 percent guaranty fee will be charged.
>
> For loans greater than $700,000, a 3.5 percent guaranty fee will be charged.
>
> The annual on-going servicing fee for all 7(a) loans approved on or after October 1, 2004 shall be 0.5 percent of the outstanding balance of the guaranteed portion of the loan. The legislation provides for this fee to remain in effect for the term of the loan.

Combination Financing

Beginning October 1, 2004, combination financing will no longer be allowed.

Prohibited Fees

Processing fees, origination fees, application fees, points, brokerage fees, bonus points, and other fees that could be charged to an SBA loan applicant are prohibited. The only time a commitment fee may be charged is for a loan made under the Export Working Capital Loan Program.

Prepayment Penalties

Effective for all loans where the applications were received by the lender on or after December 22, 2000, a new prepayment charge paid by the borrower to the SBA ("subsidy recoupment fee") has been added for those loans that meet the following criteria:

a. have a maturity of 15 years or more where the borrower is prepaying voluntarily;

b. the prepayment amount exceeds 25 percent of the outstanding balance of the loan; *and*

c. the prepayment is made within the first three years after the date of the first disbursement (not approval) of the loan proceeds.

The prepayment fee calculation is as follows:

a. during the first year after disbursement, 5 percent of the amount of the prepayment;

b. during the second year after disbursement, 3 percent of the amount of the prepayment; or

c. during the third year after disbursement, 1 percent of the amount of the prepayment.

SBA Forms

The following pages display SBA forms that may be involved in a guaranteed loan. They are displayed here to help you determine what forms you would need for the size of loan for which you are applying. When you are ready to fill in the appropriate form(s), you will find it easier to go to the SBA Web site at http://www.sba.gov/library/forms.html. At least some of the forms at that Web site allow you to fill in the forms online with computer printing, making it easier for those who review your documents. (You do, of course, want to avoid any degree of antagonizing a loan officer by submitting sloppy documents.)

List of Forms

Form 4, Application for Business Loan

Form 4a, Schedule of Collateral

Form 4-L, Loan Application up to $150,000

Form 4—Short Form, Application for Loan of $50,000 and Under

Form 413, Personal Financial Statement

Form 770, Financial Statement of Debtor

Form 912, Statement of Personal History

Form 1010, Application for 8(a) Business Development (8(a) BD) and Small Disadvantaged Business (SDB) Certification

OMB Approval No: 3245-0016
Expiration Date: 11/30/04

U.S. Small Business Administration

APPLICATION FOR BUSINESS LOAN

Individual			Full Address			

Name of Applicant Business	Tax I.D. No. or SSN

Full Street Address of Business	Tel. No. (inc. A/C)

City	County	State	Zip	Number of Employees (Including subsidiaries and affiliates)
Type of Business		Date Business Established		At Time of Application
Bank of Business Account and Address				If Loan is Approved
				Subsidiaries or Affiliates (Separate for above)

Use of Proceeds: (Enter Gross Dollar Amounts Rounded to the Nearest Hundreds)	Loan Requested		Loan Request
Land Acquisition		Payoff SBA Loan	
New Construction/ Expansion Repair		Payoff Bank Loan (Non SBA Associated	
Acquisition and/or Repair of Machinery and Equipment		Other Debt Payment (Non SBA Associated)	
Inventory Purchase		All Other	
Working Capital (including Accounts Payable)		Total Loan Requested	
Acquisition of Existing Business		Term of Loan - (Requested Mat.)	Yrs.

PREVIOUS SBA OR OTHER FEDERAL GOVERNMENT DEBT: If you or any principals or affiliates have 1) ever requested Government Financing or 2) are delinquent on the repayment of any Federal Debt complete the following:

Name of Agency	Original Amount of Loan	Date of Request	Approved or Declined	Balance	Current or Past Due
	$			$	
	$			$	

ASSISTANCE List the name(s) and occupation of anyone who assisted in the preparation of this form, other than applicant.

Name and Occupation	Address	Total Fees Paid	Fees Due
Name and Occupation	Address	Total Fees Paid	Fees Due

Note: The estimated burden completing this form is 12.0 hours per response. You will not be required to respond to any collection of information unless it displays a currently valid OMB approval number. Comments on the burden should be sent to U.S. Small Business Administration, Chief, AIB, 409 3rd St., S.W., Washington, D.C. 20416 and Desk Office for Small Business Administration, Office of Management and Budget, New Executive Office Building, room 10202 Washington, D.C. 20503. OMB Approval (3245-0016). **PLEASE. DO NOT SEND FORMS TO OMB.**
SUBMIT COMPLETED APPLICATION TO LENDER OF CHOICE

This form was electronically produced by Elite Federal Forms, Inc

Form 4, Application for Business Loan

ALL EXHIBITS MUST BE SIGNED AND DATED BY PERSON SIGNING THIS FORM

BUSINESS INDEBTEDNESS: Furnish the following information on all installment debts, contracts, notes, and mortgages payable. Indicate by an asterisk (*) items to be paid by loan proceeds and reason for paying them (present balance should agree with the latest balance sheet submitted).

To Whom Payable	Original Amount	Original Date	Present Balance	Rate of Interest	Maturity Date	Monthly Payment	Security	Current or Past Due
Acct. #	$		$			$		
Acct. #	$		$			$		
Acct. #	$		$			$		
Acct. #	$		$			$		
Acct. #	$		$			$		

MANAGEMENT (Proprietor, partners, officers, directors, all holders of outstanding stock – 100% of ownership must be shown). Use separate sheet if necessary.

Name and Social Security Number and Position Title	Complete Address	%Owned	*Military Service From To	*Sex

Race*: American Indian/Alaska Native ☐ Black/African-Amer. ☐ Asian ☐ Native Hawaiian/Pacific Islander ☐ White ☐   **Ethnicity*** Hisp./Latino ☐   Not Hisp./Latino ☐

Race*: American Indian/Alaska Native ☐ Black/African-Amer. ☐ Asian ☐ Native Hawaiian/Pacific Islander ☐ White ☐   **Ethnicity*** Hisp./Latino ☐   Not Hisp./Latino ☐

Race*: American Indian/Alaska Native ☐ Black/African-Amer. ☐ Asian ☐ Native Hawaiian/Pacific Islander ☐ White ☐   **Ethnicity*** Hisp./Latino ☐   Not Hisp./Latino ☐

Race*: American Indian/Alaska Native ☐ Black/African-Amer. ☐ Asian ☐ Native Hawaiian/Pacific Islander ☐ White ☐   **Ethnicity*** Hisp./Latino ☐   Not Hisp./Latino ☐

*This data is collected for statistical purpose only. It has no bearing on the credit decision to approve or decline this application. One or more boxes may be selected.

THE FOLLOWING EXHIBITS MUST BE COMPLETED WHERE APPLICABLE. ALL QUESTIONS ANSWERED ARE MADE A PART OF THE APPLICATION.

For Guarantee Loans please provide an original and one copy (Photocopy is Acceptable) of the Application Form, and all Exhibits to the participating lender. For Direct Loans submit one original copy of the application and Exhibits to SBA.

1. Submit SBA Form 912 (Statement of Personal History) for each type of individual that the Form 912 requires.

2. If your collateral consists of (A) Land and Building, (B) Machinery and Equipment, (C) Furniture and Fixtures, (D) Accounts *Receivable*, (E) Inventory, (F) Other, please provide an itemized list (labeled Exhibit A) that contains serial and identification numbers for all articles that had an Original value of greater than $500. Include a legal description of Real Estate Offered as collateral.

3. Furnish a signed current personal balance sheet (SBA Form 413 may be used for this purpose) for each stockholder (with 20% or greater ownership), partner, officer, and owner. Include the assets and liabilities of the spouse and any close relatives living in the household. Also, include your Social Security Number. The date should be the same as the most recent business financial statement. Label it Exhibit B.

4. Include the financial statements listed below: a,b,c for the last three years; also a,b,c, and d as of the same date, - current within 90 days of filing the application; and statement e, if applicable. Label it Exhibit C (Contact SBA for referral if assistance with preparation is wanted.) **All** information must be signed and dated.

a. Balance Sheet
b. Profit and Loss Statement (if not available, explain why and substitute Federal income tax forms)
c. Reconciliation of Net Worth
d. Aging of Accounts Receivable and Payable (summary not
e. detailed)
   Projection of earnings for at least one year where financial statements for the last three years are unavailable or when SBA requests them.

5. Provide a brief history of your company and a paragraph describing the expected benefits it will receive from the loan. Label it Exhibit D.

6. Provide a brief description similar to a resume of the education, technical and business background for all the people listed under Management. Label it Exhibit E.

Form 4, Application for Business Loan *(Continued)*

7. Submit the names, addresses, tax I.D. number(EIN or SSN), and current personal balance sheet(s) of any co-signers and/or guarantors for the loan who are not otherwise affiliated with the business as Exhibit F.

8. Include a list of any machinery or equipment or other non-real estate assets to be purchased with loan proceeds and the cost of each item as quoted by the seller as Exhibit G. Include the seller's name and address.

9. Have you or any officers of your company ever been involved in bankruptcy or insolvency proceedings? If so, please provide the details as Exhibit H.
If none, check here:
          Yes   No

10. Are you or your business involved in any pending lawsuits? If yes, provide the details as Exhibit I.
If none, check here: Yes | No

11. Do you or your spouse or any member of your household, or anyone who owns, manages or directs your business or their spouses or members of their households work for the Small Business Administration, Small Business Advisory Council, SCORE or ACE, any Federal Agency, or the participating lender? If so, please provide the name and address of the person and the office where employed. Label this Exhibit J.
If none, check here:

12. Does your business, its owners or majority stockholders own or have a controlling interest in other businesses? If yes, please provide their names and the relationship with your company along with a current balance sheet and operating statement for each. This should be Exhibit K.

13. Do you buy from, sell to, or use the services of any concern in which someone in your company has a significant financial interest? If yes, provide details on a separate sheet of paper labeled Exhibit L.

14. If your business is a franchise, include a copy of the franchise agreement and a copy of the FTC disclosure statement supplied to you by the Franchisor. Please include it as Exhibit M.

CONSTRUCTION LOANS ONLY

15. Include as a separate exhibit (Exhibit N) the estimated cost of the project and a statement of the source of any additional funds.

16. Provide copies of preliminary construction plans and specifications. Include them as Exhibit O. Final plans will be required prior to disbursement.

EXPORT LOANS

17. Does your business presently engage in Export Trade?
Check here: Yes | No

18. Will you be using proceeds from this loan to support your company's exports?
Check here: Yes | No

19. Would you like information on Exporting?
Check here: Yes   No

AGREEMENTS AND CERTIFICATIONS

Agreements of non-employment of SBA Personnel: I agree that if SBA approves this loan application I will not, for at least two years, hire as an employee or consultant anyone that was employed by SBA during the one year period prior to the disbursement of the loan

Certification: I certify: (a) I have not paid anyone connected with the Federal Government for help in getting this loan. I also agree to report to the SBA office of the Inspector General, Washington, DC 20416 any Federal Government employee who offers, in return for any type of compensation, to help get this loan approved.

(b) All information in this application and the Exhibits are true and complete to the best of my knowledge and are submitted to SBA so SBA can decide whether to grant a loan or participate with a lending institution in a loan to me. I agree to pay for or reimburse SBA for the cost of any surveys, title or mortgage examinations, appraisals, credit reports, etc., performed by non-SBA personnel provided I have given my consent.

(c) I understand that I need not pay anybody to deal with SBA. I have read and understand SBA Form 159, which explains SBA policy on representatives and their fees.

(d) As consideration for any Management, Technical, and Business Development Assistance that may be provided, I waive all claims against SBA and its consultants.

If you knowingly make a false statement or overvalue a security to obtain a guaranteed loan from SBA, you can be fined up to $10,000 and/or imprisoned for not more than five years under 18 usc 1001; if submitted to a Federally insured institution, under 18 USC 1014 by imprisonment of not more than twenty years and/or a fine of not more than $1,000,000. I authorize the SBA's Office of Inspector General to request criminal record information about me from criminal justice agencies for the purpose of determining my eligibility for programs authorized by the Small Business Act, as amended.

If Applicant is a proprietor or general partner, sign below:

By: _____

If Applicant is a Corporation, sign below:

_____

Corporate Name and Seal   Date

By: _____
           Signature of President

Attested by: _____
           Signature of Corporate Secretary

SUBMIT COMPLETED APPLICATION TO LENDER OF CHOICE

Form 4, Application for Business Loan (*Continued*)

APPLICANT'S CERTIFICATION

By my signature, I certify that I have read and received a copy of the "STATEMENTS REQUIRED BY LAW AND EXECUTIVE ORDER" which was attached to this application. My signature represents my agreement to comply with the approval of my loan request and to comply, whenever applicable, with the hazard insurance, lead-based paint, civil rights or other limitations in this notice.

Each proprietor, each General Partner, each Limited Partner or Stockholder owning 20% or more, each Guarantor and the spouse of each of these must sign. Each person should sign only once.

Business Name: ....

By: ....
      Signature and Title   Date

Guarantors:

_____   _____
Signature and Title   Date

....
Signature and Title   Date

....
Signature and Title   Date

....
Signature and Title   Date

....
Signature and Title   Date

....
Signature and Title   Date

....
Signature and Title   Date

Form 4, Application for Business Loan (Continued)

Form 4, Application for Business Loan (Continued)

Executive Orders -- Floodplain Management and Wetland Protection (42 F.R. 26951 and 42 F.R. 26961)

The SBA discourages any settlement in or development of a floodplain or a wetland. This statement is to notify all SBA loan applicants that such actions are hazardous to both life and property and should be avoided. The additional cost of flood preventive construction must be considered in addition to the possible loss of all assets and investments in future floods.

Occupational Safety and Health Act (15 U.S.C. 651 et seq.)

This legislation authorizes the Occupational Safety and Health Administration in the Department of Labor to require businesses to modify facilities and procedures to protect employees or pay penalty fees. In some instances the business can be forced to cease operations or be prevented from starting operations in a new facility. Therefore, in some instances SBA may require additional information from an applicant to determine whether the business will be in compliance with OSHA regulations and allowed to operate its facility after the loan is approved and disbursed. Signing this form as borrower is a certification that the OSA requirements that apply to the borrower's business have been determined and the borrower to the best of its knowledge is in compliance.

Civil Rights Legislation

All businesses receiving SBA financial assistance must agree not to discriminate in any business practice, including employment practices and services to the public, on the basis of categories cited in 13 C.F.R., Parts 112, 113, and 117 of SBA Regulations. This includes making their goods and services available to handicapped clients or customers. All business borrowers will be required to display the "Equal Employment Opportunity Poster" prescribed by SBA.

Equal Credit Opportunity Act (15 U.S.C. 1691)

The Federal Equal Credit Opportunity Act prohibits creditors from discriminating against credit applicants on the basis of race, color, religion, national origin, sex, marital status or age (provided that the applicant has the capacity to enter into a binding contract); because all or part of the applicant's income derives from any public assistance program, or because the applicant has in good faith exercised any right under the Consumer Credit Protection Act. The Federal agency that administers compliance with this law concerning this creditor is the Federal Trade Commission, Equal Credit Opportunity, Washington, D.C. 20580.

Executive Order 11738 -- Environmental Protection (38 F.R. 25161)

The Executive Order charges SBA with administering its loan programs in a manner that will result in effective enforcement of the Clean Air Act, the Federal Water Pollution Act and other environmental protection legislation. SBA must, therefore, impose conditions on some loans. By acknowledging receipt of this form and presenting the application, the principals of all small businesses borrowing $100,000 or more in direct funds stipulate to the following:

1. That any facility used, or to be used, by the subject firm is not cited on the EPA list of Violating Facilities.

2. That subject firm will comply with all the requirements of Section 114 of the Clean Air Act (42 U.S.C. 7414) and Section 308 of the Water Act (33 U.S.C 1318) relating to inspection, monitoring, entry, reports and information, as well as all other requirements specified in Section 114 and Section 308 of the respective Acts, and all regulations and guidelines issued thereunder.

3. That subject firm will notify SBA of the receipt of any communication from the Director of the Environmental Protection Agency indicating that a facility utilized, or to be utilized, by subject firm is under consideration to be listed on the EPA List of Violating Facilities.

Debt Collection Act of 1982 Deficit Reduction Act of 1984 (31 U.S.C. 3701 et seq. and other titles)

These laws require SBA to aggressively collect any loan payments which become delinquent. SBA must obtain your taxpayer identification number when you apply for a loan. If you receive a loan, and do not make payments as they come due, SBA may take one or more of the following actions:

- Report the status of your loan(s) to credit bureaus
- Hire a collection agency to collect your loan
- Offset your income tax refund or other amounts due to you from the Federal Government
- Suspend or debar you or your company from doing business with the Federal Government
- Refer your loan to the Department of Justice or other attorneys for litigation
- Foreclose on collateral or take other action permitted in the loan instruments.

Form 4, Application for Business Loan (*Continued*)

Immigration Reform and Control Act of 1986 (Pub. L. 99-603)

If you are an alien who was in this country illegally since before January 1, 1982, you may have been granted lawful temporary resident status by the United States Immigration and Naturalization Service pursuant to the Immigration Reform and Control Act of 1986 (Pub. L. 99-603). For five years from the date you are granted such status, you are not eligible for financial assistance from the SBA in the form of a loan or guaranty under section 7(a) of the Small Business Act unless you are disabled or a Cuban or Haitian entrant. When you sign this document, you are making the certification that the Immigration Reform and Control Act of 1986 does not apply to you, or if it does apply, more than five years have elapsed since you have been granted lawful temporary resident status pursuant to such 1986 legislation.

Lead-Based Paint Poisoning Prevention Act (42 U.S.C. 4821 et seq.)

Borrowers using SBA funds for the construction or rehabilitation of a residential structure are prohibited from using lead-based paint (as defined in SBA regulations) on all interior surfaces, whether accessible or not, and exterior surfaces, such as stairs, decks, porches, railings, windows and doors, which are readily accessible to children under 7 years of age. A "residential structure" is any home, apartment, hotel, motel, orphanage, boarding school, dormitory, day care center, extended care facility, college or other school housing, hospital, group practice or community facility and all other residential or institutional structures where persons reside.

Form 4, Application for Business Loan (*Continued*)

OMB Approval No.: 3245-0016
Expiration Date: 11/30/2004

U.S. SMALL BUSINESS ADMINISTRATION
SCHEDULE OF COLLATERAL
Exhibit A

Applicant		
Street Address		
City	State	Zip Code

LIST ALL COLLATERAL TO BE USED AS SECURITY FOR THIS LOAN

Section I - REAL ESTATE

Attach a copy of the deed(s) containing a full legal description of the land and show the location (street address) and city where the deed(s) is recorded. Following the address below, give a brief description of the improvements, such as size, type of construction, use, number of stories, and present condition (use additional sheet if more space is required).

LIST PARCELS OF REAL ESTATE					
Address	Year Acquired	Original Cost	Market Value	Amount of Lien	Name of Lienholder

Description(s)

Form 4a, Schedule of Collateral

SECTION II - PERSONAL PROPERTY

All items listed herein must show manufacturer or make, model, year, and serial number. Items with no serial number must be clearly identified (use additional sheet if more space is required).

Description - Show Manufacturer, Model, Serial No.	Year Acquired	Original Cost	Market Value	Current Lien Balance	Name of Lienholder

All information contained herein is TRUE and CORRECT to the best of my knowldege. **If you knowingly make a false statement or overvalue a security to obtain a guaranteed loan from SBA, you can be fined up to $10,000 and/or imprisoned for not more than five years under 18 usc 1001; if submitted to a Federally Insured Institution, under 18 USC 1014 by Imprisonment of not more than twenty years and/or a fine of not more than $1,000,000.** I authorize the SBA's Office of Inspector General to request criminal record information about me from criminal justice agencies for the purpose of determining my eligibility for programs authorized by the Small Business Act, as amended.

Name _____   Date _____

Name _____   Date _____

NOTE: The estimated burden for completing this form is 2.25 hours per response. You will not be required to respond to collection of information unless it displays a currently valid OMB approval number. Comments on the burden should be sent to U.S. Small Business Administration, Chief, AIB, 409 3rd St., SW, Washington, D.C. 20416 and Desk Officer for Small Business Administration, Office of Management and Budget, New Executive Office Building, Room 10202, Washington, D.C. 20503. **OMB Approval (3245-0016). PLEASE DO NOT SEND FORMS TO OMB.**

SBA Form 4, Schedule A (8-01) Previous Editions Obsolete

Form 4a, Schedule of Collateral *(Continued)*

APPLICATION FOR SBALOWDOC LOAN

OMB Approval No. 3245-0016

Expiration Date: 11/30/2004

A. APPLICANT Please Print Legibly or Type (ALL BLANKS MUST BE COMPLETED, Use "N/A," If Blank is Not Applicable)

Business Name ....

Nature of Business ....

Trade Name (if different) ....

Type: Proprietorship ☐ Partnership ☐ Corporation ☐ LLC ☐ Other ☐ (Specify)

Address (Physical Location) ....

City .... State .... County .... Zip ....

Mailing Address (if different from above) ....

City .... State .... County .... Zip ....

Phone .... IRS Tax ID # ....

Business Bank .... Checking Balance $ ....

Date Business Established ....

Date Current Ownership Established ....

Number of employees ....

Number of affiliate(s) employees ....

Total number of employees after Loan ....

Exporter? Yes ☐ No ☐ Pre-Qual? Yes ☐ No ☐

Franchise? Yes ☐ No ☐ Name ....

B. LOAN REQUEST

AMOUNT $................ Maturity: .... Purpose: ....

Have you employed anyone to prepare this application? Yes ☐ No ☐ If Yes, how much was paid? $ .... How much do you owe? $ ....

Name of Packager .... Packager's Tax ID No. or Social Security No. ....

C. INDEBTEDNESS: Furnish information on ALL BUSINESS debts. (Attach schedule if needed.) Indicate by an (*) items to be paid by loan proceeds.

To Whom Payable	Purpose	Orig. Date	Cur. Bal.	Int. Rate	Maturity Date	Pmt. Amt.	Pmt Frequency	Collateral	Status

D. PRINCIPALS: Submit a separate Section "D" for each principal of the business (including anyone who was a principal within the last six months).

D1 Full Name .... Phone .... Social Security Number .... Title ....

Address .... City .... State ...... Zip ......

Date of Birth .... Place of Birth (City, ST or Foreign Country) .... U.S. Citizen? Yes ☐ No ☐ If No, Alien reg. # ....

D2 Percentage Owned ....% **Veteran *:** Non-Veteran ☐ Vietnam Era Veteran ☐ Other Veteran ☐ **Gender *:** Female ☐ Male ☐

Race*: Amer. Indian/Alaska Native ☐ Black/Afr.-Amer. ☐ Asian ☐ Native Hawaiian/Pacific Islander ☐ White ☐ **Ethnicity*** Hisp./Latino ☐ Not Hisp./Latino ☐

*This data is collected for statistical purposes only. It has no bearing on the credit decision. Disclosure is voluntary. One or more boxes for race may be selected.

D3 **PERSONAL FINANCIAL STATEMENT:** Complete for all principals with 20% or more ownership. (currently and within the last 6 months).

Liquid Assets $ .... Ownership in Business $ .... Real Estate $ .... Assets Other $ .... Total Assets $ ....

Liabilities Real Estate $ .... Liabilities Other $ .... Total Liabilities $ .... Net Worth (less value of business) $ ....

Annual Sal. from Bus.$ .... Other Source of Repayment $ .... Source .... Residence: Own ☐ Rent ☐ Other ☐ Mthly Housing $ ....

D4 **PAST OR PREVIOUS SBA OR OTHER GOVERNMENT FINANCING:** All owners, principals, partners, and affiliates must report these debts.

Borrower Name	Name of Agency	Loan No.	Date	Amount	Balance	Status

D5 **ELIGIBILITY AND DISCLOSURES:** THESE QUESTIONS MUST BE COMPLETED. Mark "Yes" box or "No" box as appropriate.):

I. Are you or your business involved in any pending lawsuits? Yes ☐ No ☐ If Yes, provide the details as Exhibit A.

II. Do you or your spouse or any member of your household, or anyone who owns, manages, or directs your business or their spouses or members of their households work for the Small Business Administration, Small Business Advisory Council, SCORE or ACE, any Federal Agency, or the participating lender? Yes ☐ No ☐ If Yes, please provide the name and address of the person and the office where employed. Label this Exhibit B.

III. Affiliates: Do you or the applicant business have any interest in any other business as owner, principal, partner or manager? Yes ☐ No ☐ If Yes, provide details to Lender. (See Applicant Instructions.)

IV. Are you: (a) presently under indictment, on parole or probation, Yes ☐ No ☐ or (b) have ever been charged with or arrested for any criminal offense other than a minor motor vehicle violation (including offenses which have been dismissed, discharged, or knoll prosequi) Yes ☐ No ☐ or (c) convicted, placed on pretrial diversion, or placed on any form of probation including adjudication withheld pending probation for any criminal offense other than a minor vehicle violation? Yes ☐ No ☐ Cleared for Processing: Date .... By .... Fingerprints Waive: Date .... By ....

V. I have received and read "STATEMENT REQUIRED BY LAW AND EXECUTIVE ORDER".

If you knowingly make a false statement or overvalue a security to obtain a guaranteed loan from SBA you can be fined up to $10,000 and/or imprisoned for not more than five years under 18 U.S.C.1001; if submitted to a Federally insured institution, under 18 USC 1014 by Imprisonment of not more than twenty years and/or a fine of not more than $1,000,000. I authorize the SBA's Office of Inspector General to request criminal record information about me from criminal justice agencies for the purpose of determining my eligibility for programs authorized by the Small Business Act, as amended.

VI. Signature .... Date ....

E. SIGNATURE

I authorize SBA/Lender to make inquiries as necessary to verify the accuracy of the statements made and to determine my creditworthiness. I agree that if SBA approves this loan application I will not, for at least two years, hire as an employee or consultant anyone that was employed by the SBA during the one year period prior to the disbursement of the loan. And, I hereby certify that: (1) as consideration for any Management, Technical, and Business Development Assistance that may be provided, I waive all claims against SBA and its consultants, (2) all information contained in this document and any attachments is true and correct to the best of my knowledge.

Print Name .... Date ....

Signature .... Title ....

If Corporation, Attested By: ....
Signature of Corporate Secretary

SBA Form 4-L (8-01) Previous Editions are Obsolete
This form was electronically produced by Elite Federal Forms, Inc.

SUBMIT COMPLETED APPLICATION TO LENDER OF CHOICE

Form 4-L, Loan Application up to $150,000

F. LENDER   Please Print Legibly or Type **(ALL BLANKS MUST BE COMPLETED, Use "N/A," If Blank is Not Applicable)**

Name of Lender	Business Name	Applicant NAICS Code
Lender's Address	City	State	Zip
Phone	Fax	750 Agreement Date	Eligible Passive Concern Yes ☐ No ☐

G. LOAN TERMS: The following section should be completed exactly as shown in the LowDoc Program Guide.

SBA Guarantee .... % Loan Amount .... No. of Mos. to Maturity .... Payments: P&I ☐ or P+I ☐ $ .... No. of Mos. Interest Only ....
Initial Interest Rate: ☐ Fixed .... % ☐ Variable .... % Initial spread over WSJ Prime .... % Adjustment Period: Mthly ☐ Qtrly ☐ Other ☐
Life Insurance required? **Yes** ☐ **No** ☐ On Whom? .... How much $ .... Stand-by Agreements? **Yes** ☐ **No** ☐ Amount $ ....
If Start-Up or Purchasing Existing Business, Amount of Applicant Injection**: Cash $ .... Assets $ .... Stand-by Debt $ .... Other $ ....
*Equity in home is not considered injection. Provide a breakdown in Lender's Comments if the injection is in the form of assets other than cash.

Use of Proceeds:		Collateral:		Market	Existing Lien(s) *		Collateral
Amount	Purpose	Type	Description	Value	Lien holder	Balance	Value
	Acquire/Renovate Real Property						
	Acquire Fixed Assets, Non-RE						
	Impact Current Assets/Liabilities						
	Refinance SBA Debt						
	Refinance Non-SBA Debt						
	Purchase Existing Business						
	Other:						
	Total (Must equal Loan Amount)						

* If use of proceeds if for debt repayment, Lender must retain copies of refinanced notes. If for participant bank, debt refinancing may exceed 25% of total loan amount.

H. FINANCIAL STATEMENTS: (Balance Sheet and Current Income Statement must be of the same period)

BALANCE SHEET				INCOME STATEMENT			
☐ Pro Forma ☐ Interim		☐ Year End (As of ....)		No. of Interim Mos.	Prior FY	Current	Projected
ASSETS		**LIABILITIES**		**Date**			
Cash Equivalent		Notes Payable		a) Net Sales/Revenue			
Net Trade Rec.		Trade Payable		b) Cost of Sales			
Inventory		Current LTD		c) Gross Profit			
Other Curr. Assets		Other Curr. Liab.		d) Owner Comp/Drawings			
Total Curr. Assets		Total Curr. Liab.		e) Rent (if applicable)			
Net Fixed Assets		Long Term Debt		f) Depreciation/Amortization			
Other Assets		Other Liabilities		g) Longterm Debt Int. Exp.			
Total Assets		Total Liabilities		h) General & Other Exp.			
				i) Net Income after "d" above			
				A) Cash Flow (f+g+i)			
		Tangible Net Worth*		B) Total TermDebt P & I			
		*Including Stand-by debt		Debt Coverage Ratio (A / B)			

I. LENDERS COMMENTS: (Management's character, financial strength of the business, and repayment ability, including forecast. Use separate sheet if necessary.)

Business Start-Ups and Purchases: Lender **MUST** comment on management qualifications, location, competitive factors and feasibility of business plan.

J. ELIGIBILITY EVALUATION: Refer to program guide. If you have any eligibility questions, please contact to LowDoc Processing Center before submitting an application.

Eligibility Evaluation: To the best of your ability have you determined that the Borrower meets SBA eligibility requirements as outlined in the "LowDoc Program Guide" and the "Eligibility Checklist"?   **Yes** ☐ **No** ☐   (Please note, by law, SBA cannot guarantee ineligible loans.)

I submit this application to SBA for approval subject to the terms and conditions outlined above. Without the participation of SBA to the extent applied for we would not be willing to make this loan, and in our opinion the financial assistance applied for is not otherwise available on reasonable terms. I certify that none of the Lender's employees, officers, directors, or substantial stockholders (more than 10%) have financial interest in the applicant. I also certify that our institution has at least 20 qualified commercial loans outstanding demonstrating our significant experience lending to small business concerns.

Lender Officer (Print Name) ....
Signature of Lender Officer ....   Title ....   Date ....

SBA Form 4-L (8-01) Previous Editions are Obsolete

Form 4-L, Loan Application up to $150,000 *(Continued)*

INSTRUCTIONS FOR APPLICANT ON HOW TO COMPLETE THE SBA*LOWDOC* APPLICATION

The following directions provide assistance in completing the SBA*LowDoc* application. Each numbered section in this guide corresponds to the same number on the SBA*LowDoc* application. Please type or print legibly. **SBA*LowDoc* uses a credit scoring system, thus ALL application entries must be completed or use "N/A" if blank does not apply.** If necessary, use separate sheets of paper for additional answers to each section.

SECTION A: APPLICANT

1. Business Name - Legal name of the entity applying for SBA*LowDoc* loan.
2. Trade Name - The operating name, if different from business name.
3. Type - Legal organizational structure of the business.
4. Address - Street address of business.
5. City, State, County, Zip - City, state, county and zip of the business.
6. Mailing Address (if different from street address).
7. Phone - Telephone number, including area code of the business.
8. IRS Tax ID # - The business employer I.D. number assigned by the IRS, or the owner's social security number. Please do not use "**Pending**" on this line.
9. Business Bank - Financial Institution business is currently using for checking and/or loans.
10. Checking Balance - Current amount business has in checking account.
11. Nature of Business - Examples dairy farm, manufacture tires, wholesale shoes, retail toys, lawyer, etc.
12. Date Business Established - The original date the business was started.
13. Date Current Ownership Established - The date of **the most recent change** in ownership. This includes the date that the current owners acquired or purchased this business or the date of any change in the percentages of ownership of the current owners.
14. # of employees - Number of full and part-time employees on payroll for each pay period for the last 12 months averaged by the number of pay periods.
15. # of affiliate(s) employees - Please note that affiliates are defined as businesses that have common ownership, common management, or contractual relationships that give one control over the other. Calculate same as #14.
16. After the Loan - Anticipated number of employees the business will employ within two years from the date of the loan.
17. Exporter - Mark appropriate box if business exports any product or service.
18. Pre-Qual - Mark appropriate box if Pre-Qualification service used.
19. Franchise - Mark appropriate box if business is a franchise.
20. Franchise name - If business is a franchise.

SECTION B: LOAN REQUEST (Total all SBA debt, including this application, and excluding disaster loans, cannot exceed $150,000)

1. Amount - Total amount of loan requested by borrower.
2. Maturity - Number of months or years until loan is to be repaid.
3. Purpose - Briefly explain how the loan will be used.
4. Have you employed anyone to prepare this application? - Check appropriate box, amount paid, name of packager, Social Security number or Tax I.D. number of packager.

SECTION C: INDEBTEDNESS - Please provide the requested information on all business debts. NO personal debts should be listed in these blocks unless said debts were used for business purposes. Add an additional sheet if necessary. Provide the number of scheduled payments in a 12-month period or other terms, if appropriate, to report "Pmt. Frequency".

SECTION D: PRINCIPALS Complete this section for each principal. Section D can be photocopied for this purpose. **Account for 100 percent of ownership. Principal includes:** 1) the owner of a sole proprietorship; 2) each partner of a partnership; 3) each officer, director, and holder of voting stock of a corporation or a limited liability company; 4) any other person, including a hired manager, who has authority to speak for and commit the borrower in the management of the business. Non-owner officers and directors and officers owning less than 20 percent complete only parts 1,4, and 5.

Please Note: The estimated burden for completing this form is 7.50 hours per response. You will not be required to respond to collection of information unless it displays a currently valid OMB approval number. Comments on the burden should be sent to the U.S. Small Business Administration, Chief, AIB, 409 3rd Street, S.W., Washington, D.C. 20416 and Desk Office for Small Business Administration, Office of Management and Budget, New Executive Office Building, Room 10202, Washington, D.C. 20503. **OMB Approval (3245-0016).**

Form 4-L, Loan Application up to $150,000 *(Continued)*

D-1

1. Name - Full legal name.
2. Phone - Home telephone number including the area code.
3. Social Security Number - nine digit numeric.
4. Title - Position held in the business (i.e., President, Partner, etc.).
5. Address - Street, city, state, county, and zip of home address.
6. Date of Birth - Month, day, year.
7. Place of Birth - Where borrower was born, by city and state (or city and Foreign Country).
8. U.S. Citizen? - Check the proper box.
9. If No, Alien reg #. - If borrower is not a citizen, SBA must have the borrower's registration number.

D-2

1. % Owned – The percentage ownership of each owner. (The total of all must equal 100 Percent).
2. Please check appropriate boxes in this section.

D-3 Personal Financial Statement

1. Liquid Assets - Include liquid assets such as checking, savings, money markets, certificate of deposits, bonds, stocks (publicly traded), cash value of life insurance, and marketable securities. **Do not** include individual retirement accounts, and similar assets.
2. Ownership in Business - Value of ownership in the applicant business.
3. Real Estate - Market value of all real estate owned.
4. Assets Other - Any assets not otherwise listed.
5. Total Assets - Total value of all assets in numbers 1, 2, 3 and 4 of this section, D-3.
6. Liabilities Real Estate - Total of all debt/mortgages on real estate owned.
7. Other Liabilities - Total of all debt excluding real estate debt.
8. Total Liabilities - Total of all liabilities in numbers 6 and 7 of this section, D-3.
9. Net Worth - Difference between total assets, number 5, and total liabilities, number 8.
10. Annual Salary - From the applicant business.
11. Other Sources of Repayment - A Lender or SBA may rely upon a source of cash flow other than from operations of the small business borrower for repayment. That source must be available to the principal(s) on a consistent basis in an amount that sufficiently exceeds the individual's personal needs to permit orderly repayment of the loan over a reasonable period of time.
12. Source - Of other Source of Repayment in number 11.
13. Residence Rent/Own/Other - Indicate if current residence is owned, rented, or other (example, live with relatives).
14. Monthly Housing - Monthly mortgage or rent payment of residence.

D-4 - Past or present SBA or Other Government Financing-

1. Please complete for all principals. Financial Institution, Agency, Loan No., Date, Amount, Balance, and Status. (Outstanding, applied for, paid in full, and any other status.)

D-5 -Eligibility and Disclosures (IMPORTANT, only one signature is allowed in this section. USE SEPARATE SHEET FOR EACH PRINCIPAL)

Mark appropriate boxes, sign and date.

Form 4-L, Loan Application up to $150,000 *(Continued)*

INSTRUCTIONS FOR LENDER ON HOW TO COMPLETE THE SBA*LOWDOC* **APPLICATION**

The following directions provide assistance in completing the SBA*LowDoc* application. Each section corresponds to the same section on the LowDoc application. If a particular section or entry is not specified in this guide, special directions are required to complete that entry. You may find it helpful to refer to the LowDoc Program Guide if there are no credit policy questions. If necessary, use separate sheets of paper for additional answers to each section. **ALL BLANKS MUST BE COMPLETED - USE N/A IF "Blank" DOES NOT APPLY.**

SECTION F: LENDER - If you do not have the date of the latest 750 agreement, please call your SBA District/Branch Office and they will provide you with this information. The appropriate SBA District/Branch Office is based on location of business.

1. Name of Lender - Financial Institution.
2. Business Name - Applicant.
3. Applicant NAICS Code - As listed in then North American Industrial Classification System (NAICS).
4. Lender's Address - Address of Financial Institution ****IMPORTANT**** Must be street address, all loans documents are shipped FEDEX. FEDEX will not deliver to a Post Office Box.
5. Telephone - Lender's Telephone Number, including area code.
6. Fax - Lender's Fax Number, including area code.
7. 750 Date - Date of SBA Guaranty Agreement.

SECTION G: LOAN TERMS - Please complete this section as completely and accurately as possible. The Authorization for Loan Guarantee will usually be based on the terms and conditions provided, but SBA reserves the right to amend them. Any changes will be discussed prior to approval by SBA. Accuracy and completeness will expedite loan closings.

1. SBA Guarantee % - Percentage of SBA Guarantee, maximum 85 percent.
2. Loan Amount - Amount Lender has approved.
3. No. of Months to maturity - Loan maturity in months including interest only payments.
4. Payments- Mark the appropriate box if payments are principal and interest or principal plus accrued interest; enter payment. If you are asking for payments other than monthly, please indicate.
5. No. of Months Interest Only - Only if repayment terms have an interest only period.
6. Initial Interest Rate - Interest rate of the loan at closing and whether it will be fixed or variable.
7. Spread - If interest rate is variable, indicate the spread over the Wall Street Journal Prime Rate. If the adjustment period is other than monthly or quarterly, please check "Other" and indicate the frequency.
8. Life Insurance - Are you requiring principal to obtain and in what amount?
9. Standby Agreement - Who will be executing the standby and in what amount?
10. If Start-Up or Purchase of Existing Amount - Indicate nature of the source by entering the amount of the injection by the appropriate category. "Cash" is money reported on a personal financial statement. "Assets" are those assets reported on a personal financial statement. "Stand-by Debt" is any obligation which will be placed on stand-by. "Other" includes gifts, inheritances and other sources not already mentioned.

Use of Proceeds

Amount and Purpose - "Fixed Assets" includes all fixed assets financed other than real estate, such as vehicles, equipment, furniture and fixtures. "Impact Current Assets/Liability" is amount for inventory and working capital. If "Debt Payment applies, enter name and amount in space provided on application. Refinancing of participant bank debt is limited to 25 percent of loan request. "Other" include the balance of assets financed that are not specified elsewhere, such as working capital, goodwill, leasehold improvements. If the purpose of loan is to purchase a business in entirely, use "purchase of business." If only assets are being purchased use of proceeds should be itemized by asset category. .

Collateral

1. Type - Enter the code for type of collateral securing loan: RE-real estate, FF-furniture & fixtures, EQP-equipment; or INV-inventory, etc.
2. Description - Briefly describe collateral (e.g., location of real estate, type of equipment, or description of inventory).
3. Market Value - Should be the lender's assessment of the current market value of collateral. (Please note that market value should be based on prudent lending standards and values should be supported by appropriate documentation.)
4. Existing Lien(s) - If collateral is has existing lien(s), enter the lienholder name and balance outstanding on each. (Please note: enter original amount if real estate mortgage/deed of trust is open-ended.)
5. Collateral Value - Should be the lender's assessment of the collateral's liquidation value net of existing lien(s).

Form 4-L, Loan Application up to $150,000 *(Continued)*

SECTION H: FINANCIAL STATEMENTS

Balance Sheet - this section is a summary of the business' balance sheet. If the businesses is a start-up, enter a pro forma balance sheet, after application of loan proceeds. (**Use Pro Forma only if startup**).

1. As of _____ - Date of the most recent fiscal year statements if within the last three months, or the date of the most recent interim statements if not more than 90 days old at the time SGA receives the application if previous fiscal year statements are over tree months old (Note: the date of the Balance Sheet should correspond with the date of the Current Period in the Income Statement section and the date of personal financial statements).
2. Total Current Assets - Should equal the total of Cash Equivalent, Net Trade Receivable, Inventory, and Other Current Assets. Net Trade Receivables means after deduction of receivables which are unlikely to be collected.
3. Total Assets - Must equal the total of Total Current Assets, Net Fixed Assets, and Other Assets.
4. Total Current Liabilities - Should equal the total of Notes, Trade Payables, Current Portion of Long-Term Debt (Current LTD), and Other Current Liabilities.
5. Total Liabilities - Should equal the total of Total Current Liabilities, Long Term Debt, and Other Liabilities.
6. Tangible Net Worth - Net worth after deducting all intangible assets.

Income Statement - This section is a summary of the business' previous, current and projected cash flow statement. If business is a start-up, enter two years of pro forma data in the "Current" and "Projected" columns.

7. Prior FY - For period of last full fiscal year.
8. Current - Must be for the same period as the Balance Sheet Statement.
9. Projected - Over the next 12 months.
10. Rent (if applicable) - Discontinued rent due to purchase of asset(s) with loan proceeds.
11. Cash Flow - Must equal to the total of the Rent (if this expense is being eliminated), Depreciation/Amortization, Annual Interest Expense on Long Term Debt, and Net Income. (In comments. address whether the depreciation is really available for debt service on the basis of when the depreciable asset will need to be replaced.)
12. Term Debt P&I - For the Current period, enter the total of all term debt payments including principal and interest. For the projected period, enter the total of all term debt payments for the 12-month period, include the new SBA*LowDoc* loan.

SECTION I: LENDER COMMENTS - Lender's analysis of applicant's character, management abilities, financial condition of business, and repayment ability. Also any other comments you feel necessary including whether projections are realistic. Business start-ups and purchases must discuss the amount and nature of the injection of the principal(s) into the business. Lender's comments must also address whether the projections are reasonable and attainable on the basis of the applicant's capacity.

SECTION J: ELIGIBILITY - Use the SBA*LowDoc* Eligibility Checklist to assist in making and documenting the determination of the applicant's eligibility. Please keep justification for this determination in applicant's file.

Form 4-L, Loan Application up to $150,000 *(Continued)*

U.S. Small Business Administration
Application for Small Business Loan
(Short Form)
(May be used for Participation Loans of $50,000 and under)

Applicant				Address	
Name of Business				Tax I.D. No.	
Street Address				Tel. No. (Include A/C)	
City	County	State	Zip	No. of Employees (including subsidiaries and affiliates)	
Type of Business			Date Business Established	At Time of Application	
				If Loan is Approved	
Bank of Business Account and Address				Subsidiaries or Affiliates (Separate from Above)	
Amount Requested	Show how the proceeds are to be used (round to the nearest hundreds)				
Term Requested Yrs.					

The following schedules must be completed and submitted as a part of the loan application. (Applicant's name and address need only be provided once.) ALL SCHEDULES MUST BE SIGNED AND DATED BY THE PERSON SIGNING THIS FORM:

1. Include financial statements of the applicants listed below:
   ALL FINANCIAL STATEMENTS MUST BE SIGNED AND DATED.

   a. For an existing business, submit year-end financial statements, including a balance sheet, income statement and reconciliation of net worth for up to the last three full fiscal years. (Federal tax returns may be substituted for income statements.) Also submit a balance sheet and income statement for the current period (within 90 days of the filing of the application) with a summarization of the aging of accounts receivable and payable. A projection of income and expenses for one year after the proposed loan is helpful and may be requested by SBA.

   b. For a new business, prepare a balance sheet reflecting the assets, liabilities and net worth of the business assuming the loan is approved and disbursed. In addition, provide a projection of income and expenses for one year after the loan is disbursed.

2. List all assets to be pledged as collateral.

   a. For machinery and/or equipment, provide an itemized list that contains identification numbers for all appropriate items.

   b. For real estae include a legal description of the property.

   Collateral lists additionally should contain the year acquired, original cost, present market value, current balance owed, and name of lienholders. Mark this Schedule A. (SBA Form 4, Schedule A, or a computer-generated facsimile, may be used for this purpose.)

3. The following SBA forms must be submitted by each owner (20% or more ownership), partner, or officer:

   a. A current personal financial statement (SBA Form 413 may be used for this purpose),

   b. SBA Form 912, Personal History Statement. (This also may be required of hired managers who have authority to commit the business)

4. Please provide the following information (in the order shown below) for all members of management including owners, partners, officers and directors:

   Name, Social Security Number, Position held, Home Address, Percentage of Ownership (Total 100%), * Date of Entry/Discharge from Military Service, * Race (American Indian or Alaska Native, Asian, Black or African American, Native Hawaiian or Other Pacific Islander, White-Indicate one or more), *Ethnicity (Hispanic or Latino or Not Hispanic or Latino). * Sex (*This data is collected for statistical purposes and has no bearing on the credit decision.)

   In addition, provide a brief description of the educational, technical and business background for all people listed under management. Mark this Schedule B.

5. Please supply the following information (in the order shown below) on all the applicant's short-term and long-term debt. Indicate by an asterisk (*) items to be paid by loan proceeds and give reasons for payments.
   Orig. Date, Orig. Amt., Lender, Present Bal., Rate of Int., Maturity Date, Monthly Pmt., Collateral, and Current or Past Due
   (Principal balance shown should agree with the amounts on the latest balance sheet submitted.) Mark this Schedule C.

6. Please submit a signed and dated SBA Form 1624 regarding certification of debarment and suspension.

Note: The estimated burden completing this form is 0.7 hours per response. You will not be required to respond to collection of information unless it displays a currently valid OMB approval number. Comments on the burden should be sent to U.S. Small Business Administration, Chief, AIB, 409 3rd St., S.W., Washington, D.C. 20416 and Desk Office for Small Business Administration, Office of Management and Budget, New Executive Office Building, room 10202, Washington, D.C. 20503. OMB Approval (3245-0016).
PLEASE DO NOT SEND FORMS TO OMB. SUBMIT COMPLETED APPLICATION TO LENDER OF CHOICE.

SBA Form 4 (8-01) Short Form

This form was electronically produced by Elite Federal Forms, Inc.

Form 4—Short Form, Application for Loan of $50,000 and Under

COMPLETE THE FOLLOWING
INFORMATION ONLY IF IT APPLIES

7. If you have any co-signers and/or guarantors for this loan, please submit their names, tax identification/social security numbers, addresses and personal or business financial statements, as appropriate. Mark this Schedule D.

8. If you are buying machinery and/or equipment with the loan, you must include a list of the equipment and cost (as quoted by the supplier) and the supplier's name, address and telephone number. Mark this Schedule E.

9. If you, your business, or any of the officers of your business are, or have been, involved in pending lawsuits, bankruptcy or insolvency proceedings, provide the details. Mark this Schedule F.

10. If you, your spouse, any member of your household, anyone who owns, manages or directs your business, their spouses, or members of their households work for the Small Business Administration, Small Business Advisory Council, SCORE, ACE, any Federal agency, or the participating lender, please provide the name and address of the person and the office where the person is employed. Mark this Schedule G.

11. If the applicant, its owners, or majority stockholders own or have a controlling interest in other businesses, please provide their names and the relationship with your company along with the most recent year-end financial statements for each affiliate. Mark this Schedule H.

12. If the applicant buys from, sells to, or uses the services of any concern in which someone in your company has a significant financial interest, please provide details. Mark this Schedule I.

13. If the applicant or any principals or affiliates have ever requested previous SBA or other Government financing, please supply the following information: Identify the applicant, name the Government agency, date of request, whether approved or declined, original amount of the loan, present balance, monthly payments, whether current or past due, and purpose of the loan. Mark it Schedule J.

14. If anyone assisted in the preparation of this application other than the applicant, please list the name(s), occupation(s), their address(es), and total fees. Mark this Schedule K.

FRANCHISE LOANS ONLY

15. If the applicant is a franchise, include a copy of the Franchise documents available from the Franchiser(by law). Mark this Schedule L.

FOR CONSTRUCTION AND/OR RENOVATIONS OVER $10,000

16. Include, as a separate schedule, the estimated cost of the project and a statement about the source of any additional funds, other than the loan requested, for this purpose. Mark this Schedule M

17. Provide copies of preliminary construction plans and specifications. Include them as Schedule N. Final plans will be required prior to disbursement.

EXPORT LOANS ONLY

18. If loan proceeds will be used for exporting, check here _____

SUBMIT COMPLETED APPLICATION TO LENDER OF CHOICE

TO BE COMPLETED BY ALL APPLICANTS AGREEMENTS AND
CERTIFICATIONS

Agreement of Non-employment of SBA Personnel: I agree that, if SBA approves this loan application, I will not hire anyone that was employed by SBA during the one-year period prior to the application for the loan as an employee or consultant for at least two years.

Certifications: I certify:

(a) I have not paid anyone connected with the Federal government for help in getting this loan. I also agree to report any Federal government employee who offers to help get this loan approved in return for any type of compensation in the SBA Office of Inspector General, Washington, D.C. 20416.

(b) All information in this application and the schedules is true and complete to the best of **my knowledge and is submitted to SBA** so that SBA can decide whether to participate with a lending institution in a loan to me. I agree to pay for or reimburse SBA for the cost of any surveys, title or mortgage examinations, appraisals, etc., performed by non-SBA personnel provided I have given my consent.

(c) I understand that I need not pay anybody to deal with SBA. I have read and understand Form 159, which explains SBA policy on representatives and their fees.

(d) As consideration for any management, technical, and Business Development Assistance that may be provided, I waive all claims against SBA and its consultants.

(e) I have read and received a copy of the "STATEMENTS REQUIRED BY LAWS AND EXECUTIVE ORDER" which was attached to this application.

If you knowingly make a false statement or overvalue a security to obtain a guaranteed loan from SBA, you can be fined up to $10,000 and/or imprisoned for not more than five years under 18 U.S.C.1001; if submitted to a Federally insured institution, under 18 USC 1014 by imprisonment of not more than twenty years and/or a fine of not more than $1,000,000. I authorize the SBA's Office of

If Applicant is a proprietor or general partner, sign below:

By: _____ Dated: _____

If Applicant is a corporation, sign below:

_____ Dated: _____
Corporate Name and Seal

By: _____ Dated: _____
Signature of President

Attested by: _____ Dated: _____
Signature of Corporate Official

The Proprietor, each General Partner (or Limited Partner owning 20% or more), each Guarantor, each Corporate officer, each Director, each Stockholder owning 20% or more, and, where appropriate, the spouses of each of these must sign. The person signing on behalf of the business must also sign individually.

_____ Dated: _____
Signature

_____ Dated: _____
Signature

Form 4—Short Form, Application for Loan of $50,000 and Under *(Continued)*

PERSONAL FINANCIAL STATEMENT

U.S. SMALL BUSINESS ADMINISTRATION

As of _____ , _____

Complete this form for: (1) each proprietor, or (2) each limited partner who owns 20% or more interest and each general partner, or (3) each stockholder owning 20% or more of voting stock, or (4) any person or entity providing a guaranty on the loan.

Name	Business Phone
Residence Address	Residence Phone
City, State, & Zip Code	

Business Name of Applicant/Borrower

ASSETS	(Omit Cents)	LIABILITIES	(Omit Cents)
Cash on hand & in Banks	$	Accounts Payable	$
Savings Accounts	$	Notes Payable to Banks and Others	$
IRA or Other Retirement Account	$	(Describe in Section 2)	
Accounts & Notes Receivable	$	Installment Account (Auto)	$
Life Insurance-Cash Surrender Value Only	$	Mo. Payments $	
(Complete Section 8)		Installment Account (Other)	$
Stocks and Bonds	$	Mo. Payments $	
(Describe in Section 3)		Loan on Life Insurance	$
Real Estate	$	Mortgages on Real Estate	$
(Describe in Section 4)		(Describe in Section 4)	
Automobile-Present Value	$	Unpaid Taxes	$
Other Personal Property	$	(Describe in Section 6)	
(Describe in Section 5)		Other Liabilities	$
Other Assets	$	(Describe in Section 7)	
(Describe in Section 5)		Total Liabilities	$
		Net Worth	$
Total	$	**Total**	$

Section 1. Source of Income		Contingent Liabilities	
Salary	$	As Endorser or Co-Maker	$
Net Investment Income	$	Legal Claims & Judgments	$
Real Estate Income	$	Provision for Federal Income Tax	$
Other Income (Describe below)*	$	Other Special Debt	$

Description of Other Income in Section 1.

*Alimony or child support payments need not be disclosed in "Other Income" unless it is desired to have such payments counted toward total income.

Section 2. Notes Payable to Banks and Others.   (Use attachments if necessary. Each attachment must be identified as a part of this statement and signed.)

Name and Address of Noteholder(s)	Original Balance	Current Balance	Payment Amount	Frequency (monthly,etc.)	How Secured or Endorsed Type of Collateral

SBA Form 413 (3-00) **Previous Editions Obsolete**

This form was electronically produced by Elite Federal Forms, Inc.

(tumble)

Form 413, Personal Financial Statement

Section 3. Stocks and Bonds. (Use attachments if necessary. Each attachment must be identified as a part of this statement and signed).					
Number of Shares	Name of Securities	Cost	Market Value Quotation/Exchange	Date of Quotation/Exchange	Total Value

Section 4. Real Estate Owned.	(List each parcel separately. Use attachment if necessary. Each attachment must be identified as a part of this statement and signed.)		
	Property A	Property B	Property C
Type of Property			
Address			
Date Purchased			
Original Cost			
Present Market Value			
Name & Address of Mortgage Holder			
Mortgage Account Number			
Mortgage Balance			
Amount of Payment per Month/Year			
Status of Mortgage			

Section 5. Other Personal Property and Other Assets. (Describe, and if any is pledged as security, state name and address of lien holder, amount of lien, terms of payment and if delinquent, describe delinquency)

Section 6. Unpaid Taxes. (Describe in detail, as to type, to whom payable, when due, amount, and to what property, if any, a tax lien attaches.)

Section 7. Other Liabilities. (Describe in detail.)

Section 8. Life Insurance Held. (Give face amount and cash surrender value of policies - name of insurance company and beneficiaries)

I authorize SBA/Lender to make inquiries as necessary to verify the accuracy of the statements made and to determine my creditworthiness. I certify the above and the statements contained in the attachments are true and accurate as of the stated date(s). These statements are made for the purpose of either obtaining a loan or guaranteeing a loan. I understand FALSE statements may result in forfeiture of benefits and possible prosecution by the U.S. Attorney General (Reference 18 U.S.C. 1001).

Signature:	Date:	Social Security Number:
Signature:	Date:	Social Security Number:

PLEASE NOTE: The estimated average burden hours for the completion of this form is 1.5 hours per response. If you have questions or comments concerning this estimate or any other aspect of this information, please contact Chief, Administrative Branch, U.S. Small Business Administration, Washington, D.C. 20416, and Clearance Officer, Paper Reduction Project (3245-0188), Office of Management and Budget, Washington, D.C. 20503. **PLEASE DO NOT SEND FORMS TO OMB.**

Form 413, Personal Financial Statement (Continued)

FINANCIAL STATEMENT OF DEBTOR

(INSERT THE WORD "NONE" WHERE APPLICABLE TO ANY OF THE FOLLOWING ITEMS)

1. NAME	2. DATE OF BIRTH (Month, Day and Year)	
3. ADDRESS (Include ZIP Code)	4. PHONE NO.	5. SOCIAL SEC. NO.
6. OCCUPATION SBA LOAN NUMBER	7. HOW LONG IN PRESENT	
8. EMPLOYER'S NAME	ADDRESS (Include ZIP Code)	PHONE NUMBER

9. MONTHLY INCOME:	10. OTHER EMPLOYERS WITHIN LAST 3 YEARS		
	Name	Address	Dates of Employment
Salary or wages $			
Commissions $			
Other (state source) $			
Total $			

11. NAME OF SPOUSE	SOCIAL SEC. NO.	12. DATE OF BIRTH (Month, Day and Year)
13. OCCUPATION		14. HOW LONG IN PRESENT
15. SPOUSE'S EMPLOYER (Name)	ADDRESS (Include ZIP Code)	PHONE NUMBER

16. MONTHLY INCOME OF SPOUSE:	17. OTHER EMPLOYERS WITHIN LAST 3 YEARS (Of Spouse)		
	Name	Address	Dates of Employment
Salary or wages $			
Commissions $			
Other (state source) $			
Total $			

18. OTHER DEPENDENTS: _____ NUMBER			23. FIXED MONTHLY EXPENSES: (TO NEAREST DOLLAR)	
Name	Relationship	Age	Rent or House Payment	$
			Utilities	$
			Food	$
			Interest	$
			Insurance	$
			Debt repayments:	
			Household furnishings	$
19. TOTAL MONTHLY INCOME OF DEPENDENTS (Except Spouse) $			Personal Loans	$
20. FOR WHAT PERIOD DID YOU LAST FILE A FEDERAL INCOME TAX RETURN?			Automobile	$
			Doctors and Dentist	$
21. WHERE WAS TAX RETURN FILED?			Other (Specify)	$
22. AMOUNT OF GROSS INCOME REPORTED			TOTAL FIXED MONTHLY EXPENSES $	

24. ASSETS: (Fair Market Value)	(SHOW AMOUNTS TO NEAREST LIABILITIES		
Cash	$	Bills owed (grocery, doctor, lawyer, etc.)	$
Checking accounts: (Show location)		Installment debt (car, furniture, clothing, etc.)	
		Taxes owed:	
Savings Accounts: (Show location)		Income	
		Other: (Itemize)	
Cash surrender value of life insurance			
Motor Vehicles:			
Make Year License No.			
		Loans payable (to banks, finance companies, etc.)	
		Judgments you owe (Held by whom?)	
Debts owed to you: (Name of debtor)			
Stocks, bonds and other securities: (Itemize)		Small Business Administration	
		Loans on Life Insurance	
Household furniture and goods		Mortgages on Real Estate	
Items Used in Trade or Business		Margin Payable on Securities	
Other Personal Property; (Itemize)		Other debts: (Itemize)	
Real Estate: (Itemize)			
Other Assets: (Itemize)		Total Liabilities	$
TOTAL ASSETS:	$	CONTINGENT LIABILITIES	$

SBA FORM 770 (1-87) SOP 50 51 USE 3-85 EDITION UNTIL EXHAUSTED ♻   This form was electronically produced by Elite Federal Forms, Inc.   PAGE 1

Form 770, Financial Statement of Debtor

25. LOANS PAYABLE: Owed To	Date of Loan	Original Amount	Present Balance	Terms of Repayments	How Secured
		$	$	$	
		$	$	$	
		$	$	$	

26. REAL ESTATE OWNED: (Free & Clear) Address	How Owned (Jointly, individually, etc.)		Present Market Value
			$

27. REAL ESTATE BEING PURCHASED ON CONTRACT OR MORTGAGE Address	Date acquired	Balance Owed $
	Name of Seller or Mortgagor	
	Purchase Price $	Date Next Cash Payment Due
	Present Market Value $	Amount of Next Cash Payment $

28. LIFE INSURANCE POLICIES: Company	Face Amount	Cash Surrender Value	Outstanding Loans
	$	$	$
	$	$	$
	$	$	$

29. LIST ALL REAL AND PERSONAL PROPERTY OWNED BY SPOUSE AND DEPENDENTS VALUED IN EXCESS OF $200:

30. LIST ALL TRANSFERS OF PROPERTY, INCLUDING CASH (BY LOAN, GIFT, SALE, ETC.), THAT YOU HAVE MADE WITHIN THE LAST THREE YEARS. (LIST ONLY TRANSFERS OF $300 OR OVER.)

Property Transferred	To Whom	Date	Amount
			$
			$
			$

31. ARE YOU A CO-MAKER, GUARANTOR, OR A PARTY IN ANY LAW SUIT OR CLAIM NOW PENDING?
☐ YES   ☐ NO   IF YES, GIVE DETAILS

32. ARE YOU A TRUSTEE, EXECUTOR, OR ADMINISTRATOR?   ☐ YES   ☐ NO   IF YES, GIVE DETAILS

33. ARE YOU A BENEFICIARY UNDER A PENDING, OR POSSIBLE, INHERITANCE OR TRUST, PENDING OR ESTABLISHED?   NO ☐   YES ☐
IF YES, GIVE DETAILS

34. WHEN DO YOU FEEL THAT YOU CAN START MAKING PAYMENTS ON YOUR SBA DEBT?	35. HOW MUCH DO YOU FEEL THAT YOU CAN PAY SBA ON A MONTHLY OR PERIODIC BASIS?

With knowledge of the penalties for false statements provided by 18 United States Code 1001 ($10,000 fine and/or five years imprisonment) and with knowledge that this financial statement is submitted by me to affect action by the Government, I certify that all the above statement is true and that it is a complete statement of all my income and assets, real and personal, whether held in my name or by another.

Under the provisions of the Privacy Act, loan applicants are not required to give their social security number. The Small Business Administration, however, uses the social security number to distinguish between people with a similar or the same name. Failure to provide this number may not affect any right, benefit or privilege to which an individual is entitled by law but having the number makes it easier for SBA to more accurately identify to whom adverse credit information applies and to keep accurate loan records.

Any Person concerned with the collection of this information, its voluntariness, disclosure or routine under the Privacy Act may contact the Freedom of Information/Privacy Acts Division, Small Business Administration, 409 3rd St., S.W., Washington, D.C. 20416

SIGNATURE	DATE

NOTE: USE ADDITIONAL SHEETS WHERE SPACE ON THIS FORM IS INSUFFICIENT.

SBA FORM 770 (1-87) SOP 50 51 USE 3-85 EDITION UNTIL EXHAUSTED   PAGE 2

Form 770, Financial Statement of Debtor (Continued)

OMB APPROVAL NO.3245-0178
Expiration Date:9/30/2006

Please Read Carefully - Print or Type

United States of America

SMALL BUSINESS ADMINISTRATION

STATEMENT OF PERSONAL HISTORY

Each member of the small business or the development company requesting assistance must submit this form in TRIPLICATE for filing with the SBA application. This form must be filled out and submitted by:

1. By the proprietor, if a sole proprietorship.

2. By each partner, if a partnership.

3. By each officer, director, and additionally by each holder of 20% or more of the ownership stock, if a corporation, limited liability company, or a development company.

Name and Address of Applicant (Firm Name)(Street, City, State, and ZIP Code)	SBA District/Disaster Area Office
	Amount Applied for (when applicable)	File No. (if known)

1. Personal Statement of: (State name in full, if no middle name, state (NMN), or if initial only, indicate initial.) List all former names used, and dates each name was used. Use separate sheet if necessary.

   First   Middle   Last

2. Give the percentage of ownership or stocked owned Social Security No.
or to be owned in the small business or the development company

3. Date of Birth (Month, day, and year)

4. Place of Birth: (City & State or Foreign Country)

Name and Address of participating lender or surety co. (when applicable and known)

5. U.S. Citizen? ☐ YES ☐ NO
If No, are you a Lawful Permanent resident alien: ☐ YES ☐ NO
If non- U.S. citizen provide alien registration number:

6. Present residence address:
From:
To:
Address:

Most recent prior address (omit if over 10 years ago):
From:
To:
Address:

Home Telephone No. (Include A/C):
Business Telephone No. (Include A/C):

PLEASE SEE REVERSE SIDE FOR EXPLANATION REGARDING DISCLOSURE OF INFORMATION AND THE USES OF SUCH INFORMATION.

IT IS IMPORTANT THAT THE NEXT THREE QUESTIONS BE ANSWERED COMPLETELY. AN ARREST OR CONVICTION RECORD WILL NOT NECESSARILY DISQUALIFY YOU; HOWEVER, AN UNTRUTHFUL ANSWER WILL CAUSE YOUR APPLICATION TO BE DENIED.

IF YOU ANSWER "YES" TO 7, 8, OR 9, FURNISH DETAILS ON A SEPARATE SHEET. INCLUDE DATES, LOCATION, FINES, SENTENCES, WHETHER MISDEMEANOR OR FELONY, DATES OF PAROLE/PROBATION, UNPAID FINES OR PENALTIES, NAME(S) UNDER WHICH CHARGED, AND ANY OTHER PERTINENT INFORMATION.

7. Are you presently under indictment, on parole or probation?

  ☐ Yes ☐ No   (If yes, indicate date parole or probation is to expire.)

8. Have you ever been charged with and or arrested for any criminal offense other than a minor motor vehicle violation? Include offenses which have been dismissed, discharged, or not prosecuted (All arrests and charges must be disclosed and explained on an attached sheet.)

  ☐ Yes ☐ No

9. Have you ever been convicted, placed on pretrial diversion, or placed on any form of probation, including adjudication withheld pending probation, for any criminal offense other than a minor vehicle violation?

  ☐ Yes ☐ No

10. I authorize the Small Business Administration Office of Inspector General to request criminal record information about me from criminal justice agencies for the purpose of determining my eligibility for programs authorized by the Small Business Act, and the Small Business Investment Act.

CAUTION: Knowingly making a false statement on this form is a violation of Federal law and could result in criminal prosecution, significant civil penalties, and a denial of your loan, surety bond, or other program participation. A false statement is punishable under 18 USC 1001 by imprisonment of not more than five years and/or a fine of not more than $10,000, under 15 USC 645 by imprisonment of not more than two years and/or a fine of not more than $5,000; and, if submitted to a Federally insured institution, under 18 USC 1014 by imprisonment of not more than thirty years and/or a fine of not more than $1,000,000.

| Signature | Title | Date |
| | | |

Agency Use Only

11. ☐ Fingerprints Waived   Date   Approving Authority

    ☐ Fingerprints Required   Date   Approving Authority

    Date Sent to OIG

12. ☐ Cleared for Processing   Date   Approving Authority

13. ☐ Request a Character Evaluation   Date   Approving Authority

(Required whenever 7, 8 or 9 are answered "yes" even if cleared for processing.)

PLEASE NOTE: The estimated burden for completing this form is 15 minutes per re sponse. You are not required to respond to any collection of information unless it displays a currently valid OMB approval number Comments on the burden should be sent to U.S. Small Business Administration, Chief, AIB, 409 3rd St., S.W., Washington D.C. 20416 and Desk Officer for the Small Business Administration, Office of Management and Budget, New Executive Office Building, Room 10202, Washington, D.C. 20503. OMB Approval 3245-0178 PLEASE DO NOT SEND FORMS TO OMB.

SBA 912 (10-03) SOP 5010.4 Previous Edition Obsolete   ♻   This form was electronically produced by Elite Federal Forms, Inc.

Form 912, Statement of Personal History

The following is a brief summary of the laws applicable to this solicitation of information.

Paperwork Reduction Act (44 U.S.C. Chapter 35)

SBA is collecting the information on this form to make a character and credit eligibility decision to fund or deny you a loan or other form of assistance. The information is required in order for SBA to have sufficient information to determine whether to provide you with the requested assistance. The information collected may be checked against criminal history indices of the Federal Bureau of Investigation.

Privacy Act (5 U.S.C. § 552a)

Any person can request to see or get copies of any personal information that SBA has in his or her file, when that file is retrievable by individual identifiers, such as name or social security numbers. Requests for information about another party may be denied unless SBA has the written permission of the individual to release the information to the requestor or unless the information is subject to disclosure under the Freedom of Information Act.

Under the provisions of the Privacy Act, you are not required to provide your social security number. Failure to provide your social security number may not affect any right, benefit or privilege to which you are entitled. Disclosures of name and other personal identifiers are, however, required for a benefit, as SBA requires an individual seeking assistance from SBA to provide it with sufficient information for it to make a character determination. In determining whether an individual is of good character, SBA considers the person's integrity, candor, and disposition toward criminal actions. In making loans pursuant to section 7(a)(6) the Small Business Act (the Act), 15 USC § 636 (a)(6). SBA is required to have reasonable assurance that the loan is of sound value and will be repaid or that it is in the best interest of the Government to grant the assistance requested. Additionally, SBA is specifically authorized to verify your criminal history, or lack thereof, pursuant to section 7(a)(1)(B), 15 USC § 636(a)(1)(B). Further, for all forms of assistance, SBA is authorized to make all investigations necessary to ensure that a person has not engaged in acts that violate or will violate the Act or the Small Business Investment Act, 15 USC §§ 634(b)(11) and 687b(a). For these purposes, you are asked to voluntarily provide your social security number to assist SBA in making a character determination and to distinguish you from other individuals with the same or similar name or other personal identifier.

When this information indicates a violation or potential violation of law, whether civil, criminal, or administrative in nature, SBA may refer it to the appropriate agency, whether Federal, State, local, or foreign, charged with responsibility for or otherwise involved in investigation, prosecution, enforcement or prevention of such violations. See 56 Fed. Reg. 8020 (1991) for other published routine uses.

Form 912, Statement of Personal History (Continued)

Application for
8(a) Business Development (8(a) BD) and
Small Disadvantaged Business (SDB) Certification

OMB Approval:3245-0331
Expiration Date: 7/31/2004

To be completed by SBA

Date Received

Tracking #:

To be completed by Applicant

| THIS APPLICATION IS FOR | ☐ 8(a) * | ☐ SDB *only* | **CERTIFICATION** |

Firms that are 8(a) certified are certified as SDBs

NOTICE: *A firm and the socially and economically disadvantaged individuals of the firm can only participate as disadvantaged in the 8(a) program one time.*

YOUR SIGNATURE ON THIS APPLICATION for the 8(a) program INDICATES THAT YOU FULLY UNDERSTAND THIS LIMITATION AND THAT YOU HAVE NOT PREVIOUSLY USED YOUR ELIGIBILITY. Any sensitive information collected in this application is necessary to determine if applicants comply with statutory and regulatory requirements.

SECTION I:
Business Profile

Name of Firm: _____   Telephone: _____

Address: _____ E-mail: _____ @ _____ FAX: _____

City: _____ County: _____ State: _____ ZIP: _____

Primary NAICS Code: _____ PRO*Net*® Identification No: _____
(North American Industry Classification System)   Mandatory for 8(a) Certification

This firm was established on: _____   I (We) have owned this firm since: _____
                mm/dd/yyyy   mm/dd/yyyy

Dunn Number: _____

This firm is (check all applicable):
☐ A For-Profit Business   ☐ A Proprietorship   ☐ A Corporation
☐ A Partnership   ☐ A Limited Liability Company   ☐ A Broker
☐ Located in a HUBZone   ☐ DOT-Certified Disadvantaged Business Enterprise (DBE)

The average number of employees the firm (with its affiliates) had during the past 12 months was _____ . The average annual revenues for the firm (and its affiliates) during the last three years was $ _____ . The percentage of the firm's revenues earned in the primary NAICS Code is _____ %.

All applicants *must* attach a detailed explanation, including supporting documentation, noting the section and question number for each "Yes" response to the following questions:

1.	Is the firm delinquent in filing any applicable business tax returns?	[ ] Yes	[ ] No
2.	Does the firm have any past due taxes or any other delinquent Federal, state or local financial obligations outstanding or liens filed against it?	[ ] Yes	[ ] No
3.	Are there any lawsuits pending against the firm?	[ ] Yes	[ ] No
4.	Does the firm have any existing management, joint venture, indemnity, consulting, distributorship, licensing or franchise agreements?	[ ] Yes	[ ] No
5.	Have there been any changes in ownership in the past two years?	[ ] Yes	[ ] No
6.	Does the firm have an ownership interest in any other firm?	[ ] Yes	[ ] No
7.	Does any other business concern have an ownership interest in the firm?	[ ] Yes	[ ] No
8.	Does the firm buy from, sell or use the services or facilities of any other firm in which a principal of the applicant firm has a financial or any other interest?	[ ] Yes	[ ] No
9.	Has the firm or any principal of the firm previously applied for 8(a) or SDB certification?	[ ] Yes	[ ] No
10.	Has the firm or any principal of the firm received an SBA loan?	[ ] Yes	[ ] No

Form 1010, Application for 8(a) Business Development (8(a) BD) and Small Disadvantaged Business (SDB) Certification

<u>Only</u> 8(a) Applicants <u>must</u> answer the following questions and attach a detailed explanation, including supporting documentation, noting the section and question number for each "Yes" response:

11. Has the firm ever been certified as an 8(a) BD Program participant or own any assets of a previously certified 8(a) BD Program participant? [ ] Yes [ ] No

12. Does the firm have a negative net worth or working capital position? [ ] Yes [ ] No

13. Has the firm earned revenues in its primary NAICS code for less than the immediate past two years? [ ] Yes [ ] No

---

SECTION II
Business Management and Administration

Please provide the following information on all owners, directors, management members, and officers (add additional pages if necessary):

Name	Position in Firm	Percentage of Ownership Interest in Firm	Hours Devoted to the Management of firm	Access to firms Bank Account (Y/N)	Socially and Economically Disadvantaged (Y/N)

<u>All</u> applicants <u>must</u> attach a detailed explanation, including supporting documentation, noting the section and question number and any supporting documents for each "Yes" response to the following questions:

14. Does any non-disadvantaged individual or entity furnish a required license or professional certification? [ ] Yes [ ] No

15. Does any non-disadvantaged employee, owner, director, officer or management member receive compensation from the firm in any form, including dividends, that exceeds the compensation of the highest ranking officer of the firm? [ ] Yes [ ] No

16. Does any individual or entity other than the individual(s) claiming disadvantage provide financial or bonding support, office space, or equipment to the firm? [ ] Yes [ ] No

17. Is any owner, director, officer or management member a former employee or a principal of a former employer of any individual(s) claiming disadvantage? [ ] Yes [ ] No

18. Does any owner, director, officer or management member have an ownership interest in any other firm? [ ] Yes [ ] No

19. Is any owner, director, officer or management member currently a Federal employee or have a household member who is currently a Federal employee? [ ] Yes [ ] No

20. Does any owner, director, officer or management member have any delinquent Federal obligations, past due taxes or liens against him/her or his/her spouse? [ ] Yes [ ] No

Form 1010, Application for 8(a) Business Development (8(a) BD) and Small Disadvantaged Business (SDB) Certification *(Continued)*

SECTION III
Personal Information

Please provide the following information on all individual applicants who claim social and economic disadvantage
(add additional pages if necessary):

Name of Individual	Designated Group Membership or Basis of Disadvantage *	U.S. Citizenship Y/N	Place of Birth	Sex M/F	Veteran Y/N
....	....	....	....	....	....
....	....	....	....	....	....
....	....	....	....	....	....

Each individual claiming disadvantage must submit a narrative statement describing his/her economic disadvantage. Applicants who are not members of a designated group must also submit a narrative statement detailing how he/she personally experienced social disadvantage in American society <u>and</u> any supporting evidence.

Note: Applicants <u>must</u> attach a detailed explanation, including supporting documentation, noting the section and question number and any supporting documents for each "yes" response to the following questions in this section.

With respect to each individual claiming disadvantage:

21. Is any individual delinquent in filing his/her personal Federal or local tax returns?　　　[ ] Yes　[ ] No
22. Has any individual transferred any personal assets during the last two years to any immediate family member for less than fair market value?　　　[ ] Yes　[ ] No

Only with respect to each 8(a) individual claiming disadvantage (not SDB applicant):

23. Has any individual previously used his/her eligibility to qualify a firm for 8(a) BD Program participation?　　　[ ] Yes　[ ] No
24. Does any individual own individually, or in aggregate with the applicant firm and/or immediate family members, more than a 20% ownership interest in a current 8(a) BD Program participant?　　　[ ] Yes　[ ] No
25. Does any individual's immediate family member own individually, or in aggregate with other immediate family members and/or the applicant firm, more than a 20% ownership interest in a current 8(a) BD Program participant?　　　[ ] Yes　[ ] No
26. Does the applicant firm have more than a 20% ownership interest in a current 8(a) BD Program participant?　　　[ ] Yes　[ ] No
27. Has any individual ever been arrested? (If <u>Yes</u>, submit a Fingerprint Card.)　　　[ ] Yes　[ ] No

Only with respect to 8(a) applicants:

28. Does any non-disadvantaged owner of the applicant firm own individually, or in the aggregate with immediate family members, more than 10% of a current 8(a) BD Program participant?　　　[ ] Yes　[ ] No
29. Does any non-disadvantaged firm in the same or similar line of business own more than a 10% interest in the applicant firm?　　　[ ] Yes　[ ] No

* List of Designated Groups: (1)Black Americans, (2)Hispanic Americans, (3)Native Americans, (4)Asian Pacific Americans, and (5)Subcontinent Asian Americans

Form 1010, Application for 8(a) Business Development (8(a) BD) and Small Disadvantaged Business (SDB) Certification *(Continued)*

Under Title 18 U.S.C. § 1001 and Title 15 U.S.C. § 645, any person who misrepresents a firm's status as an 8(a) Program participant or SDB concern, or makes any other false statement in order to influence the certification process in any way, or to obtain a contract awarded under the preference programs established pursuant to section 8(a), 8(d), 9 or 15 of the Small Business Act, or any other provision of Federal Law that reference Section 8(d) for a definition of program eligibility shall be: (1) Subject to fines and imprisonment of up to 5 years, or both, as stated in Title 18 U.S.C. § 1001; subject to fines of up to $500,000 and imprisonment of up to 10 years, or both, as stated in Title 15 U.S.C. § 645; (2) Subject to civil and administrative remedies, including suspension and debarment; and (3) Ineligible for participation in programs conducted under the authority of the Small Business Act.

I hereby certify that the information provided in this application and supporting documents relating to the applicant, to me personally, and to my disadvantaged status is true and accurate.

By: _____   _____
    President/CEO/Proprietor/Management Member/Partner   Date

I hereby certify that the information provided in this application and supporting documents relating to my disadvantaged status and me is true and accurate.

_____   _____
Signature   Date

_____   _____
Signature   Date

_____   _____
Signature   Date

_____   _____
Signature   Date

_____   _____
Signature   Date

PLEASE NOTE: The estimated burden for completing this form is 2.5 hours per response. You are not required to respond to any collection of information unless it displays a currently valid OMB approval number. Comments on the burden should be sent to U.S. Small Business Administration, Chief, AIB, 409 3rd St., S.W., Washington, D.C. 20416 and Desk Officer for the Small Business Administration, Office of Management and Budget, New Executive Office Building, Room 10202, Washington, D.C. 20503. OMB Approval (3245-). **PLEASE DO NOT SEND FORMS TO OMB.**

SBA Form 1010 Page 4

Form 1010, Application for 8(a) Business Development (8(a) BD) and Small Disadvantaged Business (SDB) Certification (Continued)

CHECKLIST FOR PREPARING YOUR APPLICATION
(This checklist will provide basic guidelines on the attachments that you should submit with your application)
SBA will keep this information and the information provided on the application confidential to the extent required by the law.

SECTION I: Business Profile

- A detailed explanation, including supporting documentation, for each "Yes" response to questions in Section I, if applicable.
- Copies of **all** stock certificates (front and back), stock ledger, buy/sell agreements, transmutation agreements, voting agreements.
- Certificate of Good Standing (for Corporations and LLCs, if applicable).
- SBA Form 1623, Certification Regarding Debarment, Suspension, and other Responsibility Matters.
- Firms applying for SDB certification *only*, a balance sheet and profit and loss statement for the preceding fiscal year-end period.

Firms applying for 8(a)/SDB certification should submit:

- balance sheets and profit and loss statements no older than 90 days and for the preceding three (3) fiscal year-end periods,
- along with copies of the last three years of applicant firm's tax returns and schedules and attachments, and
- an executed IRS Form 4506, Request for Copy or Transcript of Tax form for firm's taxes, and
- a Statement of Bonding limit from the firm's surety, if applicable.

SECTION II: Business Management and Administration

- A detailed explanation, including supporting documentation, for each "Yes" response to questions in Section II, if applicable.
- Articles of Incorporation, Operating Agreement, By-laws, Stockholder and Board Member Meeting Minutes, Partnership Agreement, Articles of Organization, Fictitious Business Name filing, and bank signature cards.
- Copies of the business and special licenses under which the firm operates.
- Copies of loan agreements, including lines of credit and shareholder loan(s).

SECTION III: Personal Information: About each individual claiming social and economic disadvantage:

- A detailed explanation, including supporting documentation, for each "Yes" response to questions in Section III, if applicable.
- A current Personal Finance Statement on SBA Form 413 (no older than 30 days) for applicant *and* spouse, dividing all assets and liabilities as appropriate. If you are married and live in a community property jurisdiction, please provide evidence of which assets and income are community property and which are separate.
- Copies of personal income tax returns (including all schedules and W-2 forms) for the two years immediately preceding the application for the individual and spouse, and an executed IRS Form 4506, Request for Copy or Transcript of Tax Form.
- Narrative statement of economic disadvantage.
- Applicants who are not members of a designated group must submit supporting evidence of individual social disadvantage.
- Applicants for 8(a) certification must submit an SBA Form 912, Statement of Personal History (include a SBA Fingerprint Card if the SBA Form 912 reflects an arrest).
- Personal Resume, including the education, technical training and business and employment experience (employer's name, dates of employment and nature of employment), including the individual's current duties within the applicant firm.

About each non-disadvantaged principal, including each owner of more than 10%, each director, each officer, each management member, each Partner and any other individual, such as key employe, who can speak for the firm:

- Personal Resume, including the education, technical training and business and employment experience (employer's name, dates of employment and nature of employment), including the individual's current duties within the applicant firm.
- Copies of person income tax returns (including all schedules and W-2 forms) for the two years immediately preceding the application for the individual and spouse, and an executed IRS Form 4506, Request for Copy or Transcript of Tax Form.
- Applicants for 8(a) certification must submit an SBA Form 912, Statement of Personal History (include a SBA Fingerprint Card if the SBA Form 912 reflects an arrest).

Form 1010, Application for 8(a) Business Development (8(a) BD) and Small Disadvantaged Business (SDB) Certification *(Continued)*

DEFINITIONS

Immediate Family Member means father, mother, husband, wife, son, daughter, brother, sister, grandfather, grandmother, grandson, granddaughter, father-in-law, and mother-in-law.

NAICS is the North American Industry Classification System. It replaces the old Standard Industrial Classification (SIC) System. You may learn more about NAICS by accessing the Census Bureau's NAICS Internet site at: www.census.gov/naics

PRO*Net*® is the U.S. Small Business Administration's Procurement Marketing & Access Network. It is an on-line, interactive, electronic gateway of procurement information – for and about small businesses. To register for PRO*Net*® go to: http://pronet.sba.gov, select the *Register* bar and follow the instructions.

Where to Apply for Certification

For the **SDB** Certification:

U.S. Small Business Administration
Office of Small Disadvantaged Business Certification & Eligibility
409 Third Street, S.W., MC 8800, SDB 8th Floor
Washington, D.C. 20416

For **8(a) certification,** if your business is located in the following area:

Colorado, Connecticut, Delaware, Maine, Maryland, Massachusetts, Montana, New Hampshire, North Dakota Pennsylvania, Rhode Island, South Dakota, Utah, Vermont, Virginia, Washington, D.C. West Virginia and Wyoming

Please send your package to: Small Business Administration
Division of Program Certification and Eligibility
Robert N.C. Nix Federal Building
900 Market Street, 5th Floor
Philadelphia, PA 19107

Alabama, Alaska, Arizona, Arkansas, California, Florida, Georgia, Guam, Hawaii, Idaho, Illinois, Indiana, Iowa, Kansas, Kentucky, Louisiana, Michigan, Minnesota, Mississippi, Missouri, Nebraska, Nevada, New Jersey, New York, New Mexico, North Carolina, Ohio, Oklahoma, Oregon, Puerto Rico, South Carolina, Tennessee, Texas, Virgin Islands, Washington and Wisconsin

Please send your package to: Small Business Administration

Division of Program Certification and Eligibility
455 Market Street, 6th Floor
San Francisco, CA 94105

Form 1010, Application for 8(a) Business Development (8(a) BD) and Small Disadvantaged Business (SDB) Certification (Continued)

INDEX

Printed in the United States
By Bookmasters